DIS

Inside the
TOEFL® iBT

OTHER KAPLAN TITLES RELATED TO ENGLISH

TOEFL iBT with CD-ROM

Learn English through Classic Literature:
The Short Stories of Mark Twain

Inside the
TOEFL® iBT

Strategies and Practice
to Help You Score Higher

Prepared by the Professionals
at Kaplan Test Prep and Admissions

PUBLISHING
New York • Chicago

TOEFL® is a registered trademark of the Educational Testing Service, which neither sponsors nor endorses this product.

This publication is designed to provide accurate and authoritative information in regard to the subject matter covered. It is sold with the understanding that the publisher is not engaged in rendering legal, accounting, or other professional service. If legal advice or other expert assistance is required, the services of a competent professional should be sought.

Editorial Director: Jennifer Farthing
Project Editor: Anne Kemper
Production Editor: Mike Hankes
Production Artist: Virginia Byrne
Cover Designer: Carly Schnur

Published by Kaplan Publishing, a division of Kaplan, Inc.
888 Seventh Ave.
New York, NY 10106

Printed in the United States of America
October 2006

10 9 8 7 6 5 4 3 2 1

ISBN-13: 978-1-4195-9331-4
ISBN-10: 1-4195-9331-5

Kaplan Publishing books are available at special quantity discounts to use for sales promotions, employee premiums, or educational purposes. Please call our Special Sales Department to order or for more information at 800-621-9621, ext. 4444, e-mail kaplanpubsales@kaplan.com, or write to Kaplan Publishing, 30 South Wacker Drive, Suite 2500, Chicago, IL 60606-7481.

KAPLAN ENGLISH PROGRAMS

Executive Editor

Roger Frantz
Senior Project Manager
Kaplan English Programs

Developmental Editor

Liz Henly
Senior Project Manager
Kaplan English Programs

Authors

Emily Hudon, Reading
Ian Clayton, Writing
Kurt Weissgerber, Listening
Priscilla Allen, Speaking

Contributing Editors

Tom Brown
Academic Manager
Seattle Kaplan Center

Deborah Crusan, Ph.D.
Associate Professor of TESOL/Applied Linguistics
Wright State University

Emily Pierre
Academic Manager
Boston Kaplan Center

Content Editor

Jonathan Kirchherr

Production Editor

Stephen O'Connell

Executive Director of Curriculum

Kathy Charlton

Table of Contents

Part One
Introduction

Welcome!

Welcome to Kaplan's *Inside the TOEFL iBT*. This book contains 16 chapters of reading, writing, listening, and speaking practice items, strategies, explanation, and analysis that are designed to help you improve your academic English skills and get the score you want on the TOEFL iBT. Before you begin to study, it's important that you know a few things about the TOEFL, including some important changes.

THE NEW TOEFL iBT

The Test of English as a Foreign Language is a standardized test that has been designed to measure a person's ability to understand and use English as it is used in a North American university setting. TOEFL scores are used by many colleges, universities, and professional licensing organizations in the United States as a part of the admissions process. The TOEFL test is produced and administered by the Educational Testing Service (ETS), a private, not-for-profit company based in Princeton, New Jersey.

Recent changes to the TOEFL have made some test takers nervous, because the focus of the test has changed. In the past, the TOEFL focused on assessing test takers' abilities by testing specific language skills like vocabulary or grammar. Now, instead of testing what you know about English, the TOEFL expects you to demonstrate how you use English. In this book, Kaplan will show you how to understand what TOEFL questions are asking and the best way to answer them quickly and accurately.

Highlights of the New TOEFL iBT

1. **TOEFL iBT measures equally your ability to understand and your ability to produce English.** Half the total score on the test is based on reading and listening abilities—on how well you receive and understand English. Half the total score is based on speaking and writing abilities—on how well you express yourself using English.

2. **TOEFL iBT measures how well you can combine your English skills.** In the Speaking and Writing sections of the test, there are several integrated tasks, or questions in which you must read and/or listen, then speak or write based on what you read and heard.

3. **TOEFL iBT contains no Structure section.** Your knowledge of the grammar of English is measured within the skills sections of the test. For example, you must correctly apply rules of English grammar when speaking on the test.

4. **TOEFL iBT uses more authentic language in the reading and listening passages.** For example, in the Listening section, speakers in a conversation may interrupt each other, just as two people naturally do when engaged in conversation.

5. **TOEFL iBT allows note-taking.** You can, and in fact should, take notes in every section of the test.

A Map of the TOEFL iBT

Here is a map of the TOEFL iBT. The times listed below do not include the time needed to read and listen to section directions. The times listed for the Listening and Speaking sections are approximations and include the time needed to listen to conversations and lectures and to read passages. There is a five-minute break after the Listening section.

Section	Total Time	Tasks
Reading	60–100 minutes	Read 3–5 passages. Answer 12–14 questions on each passage
Listening	60–90 minutes	Listen to 2–3 conversations. Answer 5 questions on each conversation.
		Listen to 4–6 short lectures, 2 of which include student comments.
		Answer 6 questions on each lecture.
Speaking	20 minutes	Speak based on familiar experience (2 independent tasks).
		Speak based on a reading and/or a listening passage (4 integrated tasks).
Writing	50 minutes	Write a response based on a reading and a listening passage (1 integrated task).
		Write a response based on a prompt only (1 independent task).

Note that ETS sometimes includes "experimental" questions in a test to collect data on those questions so that they can be used in future test forms. For example, your TOEFL iBT may have the maximum number of reading or listening passages, because one set of questions—you won't know which—is an experimental set. If experimental questions are on your test, you will not know which ones they are, so it is important to give your best effort to every question.

TOEFL iBT SCORES

Each of the 4 sections of TOEFL iBT is scored on a scale of 0 to 30. The 4 section scores are then added together for a total test score of 0 to 120. In addition to the section scores and total score, you will receive score descriptors as part of your result. These descriptors are brief explanations of what the numeric scores mean in terms of language skills and proficiency. Most of the questions in the Reading and Listening sections are four-option multiple-choice. As you will learn in this book, several questions in these two sections are other variations of multiple-choice. Your raw scores—the total number of questions you answer correctly in these two sections—are converted into scaled scores of 0 to 30. The speaking samples you give in the Speaking section and the two essays that you write in the Writing section are all rated by human raters after you have completed your test. The scores that these human raters assign to your speaking samples and essays are then also converted into scaled scores of 0 to 30.

TEST SECTIONS

Reading

Screen Navigation and Special Features

Reading is the first section of TOEFL iBT. In the Reading section, reading passages appear on the right side of the divided computer screen, and questions appear on the left side. Because passages are long, it is necessary to scroll down to read an entire passage. The first question for a passage appears with the passage. In the Reading section, you can move forward through questions by clicking the Next button at the top of the screen, and you can move back to previous questions by clicking the **Back** button at the top of the screen. The TOEFL iBT Reading section includes a review function. Clicking the **Review** button at the top of the screen takes you to a Review screen where you can see all the questions in the section and their status— answered, not answered, not yet seen. The Reading section also has a glossary feature. A word in blue in a passage indicates that a definition is available for the word. Clicking on the word brings up this definition. A **Help** button in all sections takes you to a list of topics for which helpful explanations are available.

Reading Passages

Each passage is roughly 650 to 750 words in length. Passages generally follow the typical American English organizational structure—a one-paragraph introduction, which includes a thesis statement; body paragraphs that develop the most important points as expressed in the thesis statement; and a one-paragraph conclusion that summarizes. Some passages may vary from this structure, such as by containing an introduction that spreads over more than one paragraph.

Reading Questions

There are roughly nine different types of TOEFL iBT Reading section questions. They can be divided into two general categories, according to what each is testing: (1) basic comprehension and inference and (2) the ability to read to learn. Remember that the exact number of times a particular question type appears on a set will vary.

Basic Comprehension and Inference

These questions generally fall at the beginning of the set for a passage. Basic comprehension and inference questions constitute the majority of total Reading questions.	11–13 per set

Inferring word meaning from context	3–5 per set
Locating a referent	0–2 per set
Understanding rhetorical function	0–2 per set
Paraphrasing	0–1 per set
Understanding coherence	0–1 per set
Understanding details	3–8 per set
Drawing an inference	0–2 per set

Reading to Learn

This question generally falls at the end of the set for a passage.	1 per set
Understanding details as they relate to the main idea	1 per test (schematic table) 0–1 per set
Summarizing the most important points	0–1 per set

Listening

Screen Navigation and Special Features

Beginning in the Listening section and continuing through to the Writing section, you wear headphones that have a microphone for speaking. Once you have your headphones on, you have the opportunity to set the volume before proceeding. After the section begins, a **Volume** button at the top of the screen can be used to change the volume at any time.

You use the **OK** and **Next** buttons at the top of the screen to move through the Listening section. After choosing an answer for a question, you must click **Next** and then **OK** to proceed to the next question. The **OK** button serves to confirm each answer choice, as it is not possible to return to any question in the Listening section. While conversations and lectures play, photos of people in academic settings appear on the screen. These photos are sometimes helpful in providing context to the conversation or lecture. For example, the photo for a conversation between a student and a librarian may show two people in a library with one of them—the librarian—seated behind a reference desk. The photos do not offer any information that is directly relevant to answering the questions.

After a conversation or lecture has finished, questions appear on the screen one at a time. Each question is spoken by a narrator as it appears on the screen, though answer choices are not. A few

Listening section question types require listening again to an excerpt from the conversation or lecture. In these cases, a photo appears on the screen as the excerpt plays. A **Help** button in all sections takes the test taker to a list of topics for which helpful explanations are available.

Listening Passages

The Listening section of the TOEFL measures the ability to understand English as it is spoken in North American academic settings. The section contains:

- Two to three conversations between two people, each followed by five questions
- Four to six lectures, each followed by six questions (Note: Some lectures include student comments and questions, while others do not.)

The conversations are generally academic, between a student and a professor, or nonacademic, between a student and other university staff member, such as a librarian, counselor, administrative assistant in a university office, and so on. The conversations are often of a problem/resolution type, where the student needs assistance from the other person and must explain his or her needs in an attempt to obtain the desired assistance, and the other person attempts to assist the student. The conversations average about three minutes. The lectures are on a range of topics, but in general, all lectures fall into one of the following categories: the arts, life science, physical science, or social science. The lectures do not assume specialized knowledge, nor do they assume extensive knowledge of United States culture, government, history, etc. Lectures average four to five minutes.

Note that these lectures and passages include "authentic" language, which includes pauses, trailing off, interruptions, hesitations, false starts (e.g., "I'm not . . . I don't really know the answer to that question."), and colloquial language (e.g., "The scientists were kind of surprised by the results.") In addition, some lecturers may speak with a British or Australian accent.

Listening Questions

There are three different question types on the TOEFL iBT Listening section. You can expect to find most or all of these question types on the lectures but only some of them on the conversations. Like the Reading section questions, Listening section questions can be divided into three general categories, according to what each is testing: (1) understanding of language use, (2) basic comprehension, and (3) the ability to listen to learn.

Language Use

Understanding a speaker's implication
Understanding rhetorical function

Basic Comprehension

Identifying the main idea (lectures only)
Understanding details
Understanding purpose

Listening to Learn

Summarizing the most important points (lectures only)
Drawing an inference
Orgranizational patterns

All Listening section questions are four-option multiple-choice, with the exception of most-important-points questions. This question type comes in two formats, both of which present five options. In the first format, you must choose the three correct answers from the five choices. In the second format, you must click yes or no for each of the five options. In addition, one or two of the detail questions on lectures may ask you to choose two correct answers out of four options.

A Note about the Listening Items in This Book

Because *Inside the TOEFL iBT* does not include any audio material, you may want to ask a friend or a fellow student to read the listening transcripts that appear throughout the book. An open book icon 📖 will indicate which parts of the text should be read out loud to you.

Speaking

Section Navigation and Special Features

The first thing you must do in the Speaking section is adjust the microphone on your headset. This adjustment is done automatically as you respond to an easy question that appears on the screen.

There are six tasks in the Speaking section. In each case, you listen to directions and listen to and read the task. Two of the tasks include reading passages and a conversation or lecture, and two others include a conversation or a lecture only. For each task, you then speak for 45 or 60 seconds.

The timing throughout this section is preset. That is, unlike in the Reading and Listening sections, you do not choose when you have finished one question and are ready to move to the next. Instead, you have a given amount of time to listen to the task, prepare your response, and respond before the next task begins.

While conversations and lectures that are part of tasks play, photos of people in academic settings appear on the screen. These photos provide minimal context to the conversation or lecture. They do not offer any information that is directly relevant to answering the questions. A **Help** button in all sections takes the test taker to a list of topics for which helpful explanations are available.

Speaking Tasks

The Speaking section contains six tasks on a range of topics. Tasks 1 and 2 are independent speaking tasks—you respond to a short prompt by speaking about a familiar topic. You are scored on your ability to speak clearly and coherently. Tasks 3 through 6 are integrated skills tasks—you read and/or listen first, then speak about what you have read and heard. You may take notes while you read and listen and use your notes to help prepare your responses. You are scored on your ability to speak clearly and coherently as well as your ability to accurately synthesize and summarize the information you've read and heard.

- **Task 1: Describing something from your own experience.** This task requires a 45-second speech sample based on personal experience.
- **Task 2: Expressing and supporting an opinion based on personal experience.** This task requires a 45-second speech sample in which you give and support an opinion based on your personal experience.
- **Task 3: Synthesizing and summarizing information.** This task requires you to read an announcement, listen to a conversation about the announcement, and answer a question that asks you to synthesize and summarize information from both the announcement you read and the conversation you heard. You have 30 seconds to prepare your response, and your response should be about 60 seconds in length.
- **Task 4: Synthesizing and summarizing information.** This task asks you to read and listen to material on related topics. After reading and listening, you must give a 60-second response to a question about what you read and heard.
- **Task 5: Summarizing a conversation and expressing an opinion.** This task requires that you summarize a conversation in which two people are discussing a problem then give your opinion on a solution.
- **Task 6: Summarizing a lecture.** This task requires a 60-second summary of an academic lecture.

Writing

Section Functionality and Special Features

There are two tasks in the Writing section. The first involves listening to a lecture, so you keep your headphones on until you begin writing your essay for the first task.

Note: *Writing an essay by hand is no longer an option on TOEFL iBT. You must type both your essays. If you do not know how to type well, you should take typing lessons before taking the test.*

While a lecture that is part of the first task plays, a photo of a professor appears on the screen. This photo provides minimal context to the lecture. It does not offer any information that is directly relevant to the essay that you must write. You have the ability to cut, copy, and paste as you type your essays. A **Help** button in all sections takes the test taker to a list of topics for which helpful explanations are available.

Writing Tasks

The Writing section contains two tasks. Task 1 is an integrated skills task—you read and listen first, then write a response based on what you have read and heard. You may take notes while you read and listen and use your notes to help prepare your response. You are scored on how well you select and correctly present information from the lecture as it relates to information in the reading passage, as well as on how well you write generally. Task 2 is an independent writing task—you write an essay on a familiar topic based on a short prompt. You are scored on how well you address the topic as well as how well you organize the essay and use vocabulary and grammar.

- **Task 1: Integrated Skills.** For this task, you will have three minutes to read a passage, two minutes to listen to a related lecture, and then 20 minutes to write your response.
- **Task 2: Writing.** For this task, you will have 30 minutes to write about a familiar topic.

KAPLAN'S TOP 5 TEST DAY STRATEGIES

Remember, with your hard work and the strategies in this book, Kaplan will help you get the TOEFL score you want!

1. **Register early!** Spaces at TOEFL testing centers fill up quickly. The TOEFL iBT has been available in the United States since September 2005. You can register to take the TOEFL test in several ways:

   - Register online at least seven days before an exam using the Educational Testing Service Web site at *www.toefl.org*.

   - Call 800-GO-TOEFL at least seven days before an exam if you plan to take the test in the United States, Canada, or U.S. Territories. Call 443-751-4862 if you live outside the United States and plan to take the TOEFL at a center inside the United States. Or to take a test outside of the United States, Canada, or U.S. Territories, call the Regional Registration Center for the country where you plan to take the test (800-529-3590 TTY).

   - To take a test in the United States, mail a completed TOEFL iBT Registration Form to: ETS-TOEFL iBT Registration Office, PO Box 6152, Princeton, NJ 08541, USA. Note: Registration by mail must be received by ETS at least four weeks before an exam.

   - To take a test outside the United States, refer to the Registration Bulletin for more information.

2. **Know where the testing center is and plan a route to get there early.** Avoid putting extra stress on yourself by making sure that you know where you need to go ahead of time.

3. **Make sure that you bring proper identification and documentation.** Identification requirements vary depending on your testing location. For specific information about required identification documents, please check the information that applies to you by visiting the ETS TOEFL Web site.

4. **Prepare for test day.** The TOEFL takes a long time. Make sure that you eat well and get a good night's sleep before you take the test. Although there is a five-minute break after the Listening section, it's probably a good idea to use a bathroom before the test begins.

5. **Last but not least:** Relax! If you have worked through this book, you have seen the types of questions that the TOEFL will ask you and practiced strategies to answer them accurately.

Now you're ready to begin studying for the TOEFL iBT!

Part Two
Basic Skills

Part Two of the book covers the basic skills and strategies that you will need for reading, writing, listening, and speaking on the TOEFL test. To get the most out of this part, be sure that you complete all of the practice exercises and sample questions in each chapter.

Chapter 1:
Reading: Introduction to a Passage

Before we review some reading strategies, let's take a look at the reading passages you will find in the Reading section of the TOEFL. TOEFL reading passages follow the typical organizational structure of academic English: first the introduction, then the body paragraphs, and finally the conclusion.

Introduction to a Passage

Let's start with the beginning of the reading passage: the introduction. Reading the introduction carefully can help you to get important general information about the passage. While you are reading the introduction, ask yourself the following questions:

- **What is the topic of the passage?** The first sentence in the introduction of a passage will often state the topic of the reading. Once you discover what the passage is generally about, you will be better prepared to decide what information is most important in the passage.

- **Are the remaining sentences in the introduction more general or more specific than the first sentence?** If the sentences are more specific, they will provide detailed information about the topic of the passage.

- **What is the thesis of this passage?** A thesis statement introduces the main idea that the reading passage will develop. The last sentence in the introduction is often a thesis statement.

If you ask yourself these questions as you read the introduction, you will quickly be able to discover the topic and thesis of the passage, how the passage is organized, and the function or purpose of the passage before you have even read the entire passage.

The Body Paragraphs of a Reading Passage

The introduction is followed by several *body paragraphs*. These paragraphs will present, support, and develop the most important points of the passage. While you are reading the body paragraphs, ask yourself the following questions:

- **What is the topic of this paragraph?** As you read, remember that the first sentence of a paragraph often, but not always, states the topic of the paragraph. If you can determine the topic of the paragraph, you will be better prepared to decide what information is most important in the paragraph.

- **What are the most important points in this paragraph?** After the topic sentence, the remainder of each body paragraph presents key details that support the topic. These details will help you understand the whole passage.

If you ask yourself these questions as you read the body paragraphs, you will be able to learn about the most important details in the passage, as well as the organization and the function of the passage.

The Conclusion of a Reading Passage

The final paragraph of a reading passage is usually the conclusion. This is not always true—occasionally a conclusion can be the last few sentences of the final body paragraph. However it appears, the conclusion of a passage summarizes the most important points from the passage. It does not contain any new information about the topic. Reading the conclusion carefully will point you to the topic, important points, and thesis of the passage.

Rhetorical Function

As you read, it is important that you ask yourself: **What is the purpose** of this passage? The **rhetorical function** of a reading passage is the specific purpose of the passage. This refers to how the author intends to persuade the reader that the content of the writing is sound and believable. Some of the ways that an author might have written a passage to convince the reader include:

- Defining
- Describing
- Exemplifying
- Explaining

It is important that you understand what rhetorical function is, because each TOEFL Reading passage includes up to two questions on this topic.

READING STRATEGIES

Now that you know the basics of the TOEFL Reading section, it's time to cover some reading strategies.

Skimming

Skimming means reading very quickly to find the important points of a passage without focusing on specific details. Skimming a reading passage is an efficient way to determine the main idea, most important points, organization, and the rhetorical function of a text. Effectively skimming a passage can help you to do the following:

- Identify the thesis statement and topic sentences of the passage
- Recognize the basic organization of the passage
- Take note of repeated key words in the passage

Because the TOEFL is a timed test, you probably won't have enough time to read through every passage thoroughly, so skimming is an essential skill for you to build.

Note-Taking

Taking notes as you read is the best way to keep track of the information you process as you skim. There are many different ways to take notes. Each way can be used with different types of texts or for different parts of a text. One way that can be useful when taking notes from a descriptive text, such as the following "Recovery of the Gray Wolf," is the clustering method. In this method, you note down one main idea in a center circle, then add supporting points around it. Read the following passage and then study the following note-taking example.

Recovery of the Gray Wolf

At one time in North America, wolves ranged from coast to coast and from Canada to Mexico—the greatest natural range of any mammal except humans. Unfortunately, in industrialized human society, wolves seem to have met their match. Gray wolves began declining in the American West around 1870 as westward-moving settlers depleted the bison, deer, and elk that wolves preyed on. Wolves then turned to sheep and cattle as prey. Settlers and government trappers responded with intensive campaigns to wipe out the wolf. Approximately 1.5 million wolves were killed in various bounty-hunting campaigns carried out between 1850 and 1900. As recently as 1965, hunters were offered 20 to 50 dollars for every wolf they could kill.

Human incursions on their habitat and purposeful extermination campaigns had a devastating effect. Except for a small number of wolves in Minnesota, wolves were gone from the 48 states of the continental United States by the late 1920s. Wolves were listed as endangered in 1973 and remain so today, meaning that they are in danger of becoming extinct in all or part of their natural habitat.

However, there are some hopeful signs of a recovery in the wolf population. In the 1980s, wolves began appearing in Montana, apparently having migrated from Canada. There are currently about 65 wolves in northwestern Montana. The work of the U.S. Forest Service in augmenting the wolf population in the continental United States with wolves from Canada could speed the recovery process. In the 1990s, Forest Service employees released eight Canadian gray wolves in Yellowstone National Park and four in central Idaho. The goal was to have 10 breeding pairs and their young—about 100 wolves—in each of three recovery areas (northwest Montana, central Idaho, and the Yellowstone National Park area) by the early 21st century.

The wolf recovery program has been more success-ful than many people had anticipated. In 2003, a Forest Service survey determined that the gray wolf population had successfully settled into many of its new habitats. The survey counted 30 breeding pairs of wolves well distrib-uted throughout the three states of Idaho, Montana, and Wyoming. The indication that the wolf population was able to sustain itself allowed the federal government to change the status of the gray wolf from "endangered" to "threatened" in some parts of the western United States. While the wolves still require monitoring and protection, it appears that the gray wolf may be on the road to recovery.

Humans had devastating effect on habitat

Listed as endangered in 1973

Wolves gone from continental U.S. by 1920's (except Minnesota)

Still in danger of becoming extinct in wild

Summarizing

Summarizing is an essential skill for success on the TOEFL. Taking good notes is a very important part of summarizing, whether you are reading a long text in the Reading section, listening to a lecture or a conversation in the Listening section, or reading or listening to shorter passages in the Speaking and Writing sections. You will also need to summarize when you perform several of the tasks in the Speaking and Writing sections.

To summarize any type of reading passage you need to understand two important things:

1. What is the main idea?

2. Which supporting details are the most important?

Summarizing is a critical skill, so take the time to practice it now. Read the following short passage and then study the sample summary.

Announcement from the English Department

Due to a recent increased interest in the works of Jack Kerouac, the English department is pleased to offer a new course beginning spring quarter. This advanced class will focus on lesser-known works of this great American writer. Materials to be covered may include *Dharma Bums*, *Visions of Cody*, and Kerouac's personal letters and journal writings. This class will be open only to English majors in their third or fourth year and will meet twice a week. For more information about the content and schedule of this course, please contact Professor Carlson in Office 312.

Sample Summary

The English Department is offering a new course this spring to third- and fourth-year English majors. The course will cover lesser-known writings of Jack Kerouac and will meet twice a week. For more information, contact Professor Carlson in Office 312.

PRACTICE: READING QUESTIONS

Knowing how to identify the different TOEFL question types is important for understanding how and where you can apply the strategies in this book.

There are several question types on the Reading section of the TOEFL. Three are:

1. Drawing an inference

2. Summarizing the most important points

3. Understanding rhetorical function

Recognizing these question types and understanding what each of these types is testing is very important to getting a better TOEFL score.

Question Type 1: Drawing an Inference.

There are three to five passages in the Reading section of the TOEFL, each followed by up to two *drawing an inference* questions.

As you have learned, skimming is a process that can help you identify the main idea and most important points in a passage, and taking notes can help you organize this information.

Refer back to the reading passage titled "Recovery of the Gray Wolf."

Some drawing an inference questions ask you about the main idea. However, questions are not phrased like this: "What is the main idea of this passage?" Instead, part of the main idea is presented in the question, and part is presented in an answer choice.

A TOEFL drawing an inference question on the "Gray Wolf" passage might look like this:

According to the passage, the gray wolf

(A) has recovered most of its former range.

(B) only existed in Minnesota.

(C) was nearly hunted to extinction in the United States.

(D) killed all of the livestock of early American settlers.

Based on your reading of "Recovery of the Gray Wolf," which answer is correct?

Answer: When a test maker creates a multiple-choice question, the incorrect answer choices are generally written so as to appear to be correct to some test takers. If the incorrect answer choices were all obviously wrong, every test taker would get most or all questions correct, and the test would not effectively measure anything. Incorrect answer choices are designed to distract test takers from the correct answer, and for this reason they are called distracters.

The distracters in main idea questions do not correctly express the main idea when joined to the information in the question. The gray wolf was in fact recovering in several different sections of its previous range, but not everywhere from Canada to Mexico or from the east to west coast of the United States, so it is incorrect to say that the gray wolf has recovered most of its former range. Choice (A) is a distracter. At one point the passage states that the gray wolf was limited to Minnesota in the continental United States, but the passage does not state that the wolf was missing from Canada or Alaska. Choice (B) is also a distracter. The passage states that the gray wolf killed some of the livestock of early settlers after other food became scarce, but there is no indication that all of the livestock was killed by wolves. Choice (D) is also a distracter. The gray wolf was in fact nearly hunted to extinction in the United States, so choice (C) is correct.

Question Type 2: Summarizing the Most Important Points

There are three to five passages in the Reading section of the TOEFL, each of which may be followed by a *most-important-points* question.

Some TOEFL reading questions require you to summarize the most important points in the passage by choosing three sentences from a list of six. To answer this type of question correctly, you will need to skim and take notes as well as use your summarizing skills to determine the important points of the passage quickly. You will also need to avoid distracters, answers that may seem right at first but are not.

The types of distracters for this type of question include:

- Answer choices that express ideas that are not mentioned in the passage
- Answer choices that express ideas that are only minor points in the passage

Look at the following example of a most-important-points TOEFL question. It will require you to re-read the "Gray Wolf" passage.

An introductory sentence is provided here as a brief summary of the passage. Complete the summary by selecting the THREE answer choices that express the most important ideas in the passage. Some sentences do not belong in the summary, because they express ideas that are not presented in the passage or are only minor ideas in the passage.

The gray wolf population in the continental United States is beginning to return from the brink of extinction.

Answer Choices

- As recently as 1965, hunters were offered between 20 to 50 dollars for every wolf they could kill.
- The United States Forest Service and other groups have worked to reintroduce the gray wolf into the wild, and it seems as though the population is recovering.
- In the 1980s, wolves began appearing in Montana, apparently traveling south from Canada.
- Eventually gray wolves were hunted to near extinction and declared an endangered species.
- While it used to have a range from Mexico to Canada, the gray wolf found it difficult to compete with new settlers as they moved westward.
- The federal government was able to change the status of the gray wolf from endangered to threatened.

Answer: The three correct answers are:

1. While it used to have a range from Mexico to Canada, the gray wolf found it difficult to compete with new settlers as they moved westward.

2. Eventually gray wolves were hunted to near extinction and declared an endangered species.

3. The United States Forest Service and other groups have worked to reintroduce the gray wolf into the wild, and it seems as though the population is recovering.

Question Type 3: Understanding Rhetorical Function.

There are three to five passages in the Reading section of the TOEFL, each followed by up to two rhetorical function questions.

Another type of question in the Reading section of the TOEFL asks about rhetorical function. As mentioned earlier, writers often use rhetorical functions such as defining, describing, exemplifying, and explaining to support their main ideas.

Rhetorical Function Question Forms

Two forms of rhetorical function questions can be found on the Reading section of the TOEFL. The first form presents the rhetorical device and asks its function. Look at the example of the first form, and answer the question.

Why does the author mention the Yellowstone National Park in paragraph three of the passage?

Ⓐ To define the term *recovery process*

Ⓑ To describe a typical recovery area

Ⓒ To give an example of somewhere the wolf population was being augmented

Ⓓ To explain why the Forest Service was working to increase the gray wolf population

---

Answer: Paragraph two of the passage describes the effect that human beings had on wolf populations in the continental United States. Paragraph three discusses repopulation programs as a way of demonstrating the government's response to the near extinction of the gray wolf described in paragraph two. Choice (C) is correct. Although the wolves were reintroduced in Yellowstone, that was not the only location where the reintroduction took place, so paragraph three does not serve the function of defining the term, so choice (A) is a distracter. Paragraph three does not really describe what a recovery area is, so choice (B) is also a distracter. Choice (D) is likewise a distracter, because the paragraph does not explain why the Forest Service was working to increase the gray wolf population.

The second form of this question type presents the rhetorical function and asks how it is achieved. Look at the example of the second form and answer the question.

In paragraph four, the author describes the recent changes in wild gray wolf populations by

   (A) arguing that the population numbers are growing

   (B) identifying growth within a specific wolf pack

   (C) listing several states with growing wolf populations

   (D) comparing increases in pack size between different wolf populations

---

Answer: Paragraph four describes successful population growth in several different states, so choice (C) correctly answers how the rhetorical function in question is achieved.

To answer questions about rhetorical function correctly, you will also need to avoid distracters. Distracters for this type of question include:

- Answer choices that use words from the passage in a way that is not connected to the question
- Answer choices that are untrue based on the information in the passage
- Answer choices that express ideas that are not mentioned in the passage
- Answer choices that cite an unrelated rhetorical function or device

Answer the following practice question on determining which types of distracters have been used for each incorrect answer choice.

> In paragraph four of the passage, why does the author mention the 30 breeding pairs of gray wolves?
>
> (A) To explain how the wolves have adapted to their new surroundings
>
> (B) To describe the general atmosphere during the Civil War
>
> (C) To compare the recovery efforts between Idaho, Montana, and Wyoming
>
> (D) To give an example of the federal government changing an endangered species' status to "threatened"

Types of Distracters

_____

_____

_____

Answer: In the final paragraph of the passage, the author explains how the population recovery efforts of the U.S. Forest Service created a self-sustaining population of wild wolves in Idaho, Montana, and Wyoming. The author is not describing the adaptation of the wolves to their new surroundings, so choice (A) presents an unrelated rhetorical function. The author mentions the states Idaho, Montana, and Wyoming in paragraph four, but only to define the range of the successful breeding wolf pairs, not to compare the states to each other. Choice (D) uses words drawn directly from the fourth sentence of paragraph four but not in a way that answers the question.

Now that you have reviewed some reading strategies, let's move on to some writing strategies.

Chapter 2:
Writing: The Descriptive Essay

There are two tasks in the Writing section of the TOEFL. In the first, you must read a passage, listen to a lecture, then write an essay about what you have read and listened to. In the second, you must write an essay based only on a short prompt that asks you to describe or explain something or to express and support your opinion on an issue. In this chapter we will focus on the second type of essay.

For this essay, you do not need any specialized knowledge. The question will be based on topics that will be familiar to all test takers. You are given 30 minutes to plan, write, and revise this essay. Typically, an effective essay will contain a minimum of 300 words. Essays will be judged on the following:

- The quality of the writing, including idea development and organization
- The quality and accuracy of the language used to express these ideas

When you begin either writing task on the TOEFL, always read the prompt carefully to make sure that you know exactly which essay type you are being asked to write.

Recognizing Descriptive Essay Prompts

Now let's take a look at how to answer a descriptive essay question. The most important function of a descriptive essay is to provide information. The second function is to explain that information so that the reader can best understand it. A descriptive essay is not intended to argue a point or defend an opinion.

What does the prompt for a descriptive essay look like? Look at the following examples:

- What do you consider the distinctive qualities of a good teacher to be?
- Identify and describe the most visited geographical feature of your country.
- In your opinion, what has been the most important event of the last ten years? Describe the event, supporting your answer with specific details.

The active verbs in these prompts include *consider, identify,* and *describe.* All of them are asking you to provide an explanation and details about a particular topic to help the reader to understand it better. That is the function of a descriptive essay.

Planning a Descriptive Essay

Good planning is essential to successful essay writing. Even experienced writers make careful plans before beginning to write.

There are several steps to planning an essay. All of them should be followed closely; following them will help you write your essay more easily. Here is a list of steps you should use to help you write a better essay.

1. Read the test question (or the assignment) very carefully to make sure you understand what it is asking you to do.

2. Consider the topic thoroughly.

3. Brainstorm ideas about the topic.

4. Evaluate your ideas and select those that will best help you respond to the prompt or assignment.

5. Organize your ideas in the order you wish to present them. (This is sometimes called outlining.)

6. Identify and list details, examples, and other supporting information you can use with each of the ideas in your list.

7. Write your introduction.

8. Write your body paragraphs.

9. Write your conclusion.

10. Revise, edit, and proofread.

Note that at any point you can go back to an earlier step if you need to. Let's explore some of these steps in greater detail.

Brainstorming

Brainstorming is a process that you use to generate ideas about a topic before you actually begin writing. If you have lots of ideas down on paper, you can think about each of them, map out how they best fit together, and decide which ones you actually want to use in your writing. With practice, you will learn how to use brainstorming quickly and efficiently to prepare to write an essay answer for the TOEFL.

There are several techniques for brainstorming. They are sometimes referred to as *listing, clustering,* and *freewriting*.

Listing

Listing is a good technique for getting lots of ideas on paper quickly. All you need to do is write down every idea related to the topic that comes into your head. It isn't necessary to stop and consider each one—the main thing is just to get lots of ideas written down.

Here is a prompt and the a list one writer generated in response to it:

Prompt: "What are the most important impacts of airplanes on society?"

- Fast
- Technology innovations
- Noise pollution
- High fuel cost
- Space travel
- Military power

- Increased travel for non-rich
- diseases travel faster
- economic importance
- increased trade
- convenience
- accidents and crashes

At this point, you may decide to divide the list into positive and negative impacts. Another option is to list only the social effects: the importance of airplanes to the national economy, the pollution they cause, and the harm done by the accidents that happen every year. Alternatively, you could select only those with which you have personal experience. It's up to you to rank, organize, or rearrange your list.

Clustering

One method of brainstorming is called clustering. Clustering is much like listing, except that it allows you to begin organizing your ideas as you think of them. You begin with just a few central ideas, then link each new idea as you think appropriate. For example:

- Negative: noise, diseases travel, accidents and crashes
- Positive: economic importance, increased travel, increased trade

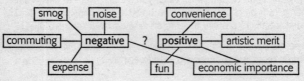

Freewriting

Another brainstorming technique is called freewriting, and it works just the way it sounds. You put pen to paper and start writing about the topic, putting down whatever thought comes into your head, until enough good ideas take shape to write the essay.

There are two important things to remember about freewriting. First, don't worry about grammar and spelling. Those can be taken care of later. Second, don't stop writing until you're finished. It's important to let your thoughts keep flowing.

In the following freewriting example, notice how the thoughts flow freely from one to another:

> Impacts of airplanes on society, well, there are lots, there's the cost of owning an airplane, or the cost of buying a ticket if you don't, fuel, maintenance, and so on, they also crash now and then, there's the loud noise from engines when they take off or land, all the space that is

required by airports, and most people still have to drive
to an airport before they can fly anyway, but I'm only
thinking of negative things—let's see, they're sure convenient, and they can take a lot people great distances
very quickly, and some them are really quite beautiful, and
can be collector's items, and building them sure provides
a lot of jobs for people. But the noise is a real problem for
people who live near airports . . . .

From this, you can draw lots of ideas for an essay. Freewriting also offers the advantage of allowing you to begin to experiment with expressing your ideas in phrases and sentences.

Outlining

Once you have generated enough good ideas for writing your essay, the next step is to organize them and to provide supporting details.

A good way to plan your essay is to prepare an outline. An outline is a chart that shows exactly how the essay is to be organized, giving you a kind of blueprint to use as you write. This way you won't wander away from your topic, get distracted, or forget what you were going to say next.

In an outline, each subsection is listed in order using Roman numerals, and supporting ideas will be listed under each subsection using the alphabet.

Here is an outline for an essay about the impact of airplanes. If this were an outline for a 30-minute TOEFL essay, each Roman numeral would represent one paragraph of writing.

  I. Introduction
 II. History
     A. Early attempts
     B. The Wright brothers
     C. Early successes
III. The airplane goes to work
     A. Access for the public
     B. Military

     C. Economic
        1. Mail delivery
        2. The travel industry
 IV. Conclusion

An even more detailed outline could possibly be prepared, including all the supporting information and examples the author intends to use. It's not necessary to use so much detail, however—an outline like this one, which uses just the main ideas and the supporting details, can be very helpful on its own. Nor is it necessary to use all the numbers and letters exactly the way they are used here—just make sure that you can understand what the outline is telling you.

Finally, don't imagine that just because you've drawn an outline, you have to follow it exactly. As you write, you may change your mind about how to organize the essay. That's not a problem—just adjust the outline to reflect your changes.

Now that you have studied and practiced planning an essay, you are ready to work on writing your essay.

Writing the Introduction to a Descriptive Essay

Like any essay, a descriptive essay should be composed of several identifiable parts, each with its own specific function. These parts usually include an introduction, a body, and a conclusion. First, we will focus on the introductory paragraph.

You may recall some information about introductions from Chapter 1 on reading. Remember, an introduction must accomplish several tasks. First, it should introduce the topic of the essay. Ideally, this can be achieved in an interesting manner that catches and holds the reader's attention, which is a rhetorical device called a *hook*. Second, an introduction must provide some context for the discussion, including any background information the reader may need to understand the essay as whole. Third, an introductory paragraph to a descriptive essay should provide the reader with a good idea of the topics that will be addressed in the essay and the order in which they will appear. This function is called *forecasting*, and it is accomplished in a thesis statement. Let's review these in greater detail.

The Hook

A hook can take several forms. It might be a fascinating fact; a provocative, emotionally charged statement; a new interpretation of an accepted fact; or even a few sentences that briefly describe an event related to the essay's topic. Whatever its form, the hook's main function is to attract the reader's attention and make him or her want to read further.

Background Information

Once you have gotten the reader's attention with the hook, the rest of the introductory paragraph can then provide any necessary background information. Some of this may have already been provided in the hook. Don't try to include too much information in your introduction. It is important to provide enough information here to introduce the topic but not so much that the introduction becomes a part of the discussion itself. When you write the introductory paragraph, you may need to answer some of these questions:

- Why is this topic important?
- What background information does the reader need before reading further?
- What did I choose to write about this topic?

Definitions are often helpful in introductions, especially when you suspect that readers may initially misunderstand the topic. You may also want to tell your reader what sources you used to find the information you put in the essay.

The Thesis Statement

The last sentence or two of the introduction to an essay is usually used to tell the reader what to expect from the essay, or to forecast. You can think of it as a kind of table of contents for the essay: a list of topics and the order in which they occur. For shorter essays, you can simply list the topic of each paragraph of your discussion. Or, if your essay is divided into more general subsections, you can refer to the main idea of each of the subsections.

Writing the Body Paragraphs

When you have finished your introduction and have written your thesis statement, the next step is to write *body paragraphs.* A body paragraph has two main parts.

The Topic Sentence

The first part, the *topic sentence,* introduces the main idea that the paragraph will discuss. It also provides supporting details, which explain the topic. Usually, a topic sentence is a general comment about the idea that paragraph will discuss. Sometimes you can include a closing sentence, or a transition to the next paragraph, though these are not always necessary. Can you see how a body paragraph looks a lot like a mini-essay?

Supporting Details

Supporting details can also take a variety of forms. Typically, these can be descriptions, explanations, definitions, examples, or a mixture of the four. In all cases, the supporting information should include specific discussion of the idea introduced in the topic sentence and should be carefully chosen to help the reader understand the topic. A paragraph should never include information that is not directly related to its topic.

When describing an aspect of your topic, try to use words that are carefully chosen to carry the most information in the least space. Efficiency is important in timed writing. Remember, your goal is to help your readers understand, not to overwhelm them with unimportant details.

The same is true of explanations. If your topic requires a reference to complex processes, mechanisms, or systems, supply only enough information to help your reader understand how this fits into the topic as a whole and no more. Too much information can quickly become exhausting for the reader, and writing down every detail takes up your valuable time.

Definitions are most useful when you suspect that the reader may be unfamiliar with a particular term or label that is a key part of your essay. If you provide a definition the first time a potentially confusing term appears in your essay, you are making sure that your reader understands what you are writing about.

Examples are the most important kind of supporting detail you can provide. Beginning writers often fail to use them enough. A well-chosen example can turn a weak argument into a strong one, help to convince a skeptical reader, and add a measure of interest and color to an otherwise dull discussion.

PRACTICE: ESSAY WRITING

Following is an example of the second task in the Writing section of the TOEFL. Once you have written your essay, spend at least 15 minutes evaluating it according to the principles outlined in this chapter.

Read the essay topic that follows. You have 30 minutes to plan, write, and revise your essay. Typically, an effective response will contain a minimum of 300 words.

Describe one event from your country's history and explain why it was important. Provide clear explanations and details in support of your answer.

Answer: Responses will vary, but here is one example of an essay.

Sample Descriptive Essay

The Dred Scott decision was an important milestone in the history of pre–Civil War America. Dred Scott was a slave, born in the late 18th century, in Southampton County, Virginia. When he was about 30 years old, his master took him from Missouri, a slave state, to Illinois, a free state, then to the free Wisconsin territory, and finally back to Missouri. Once they had settled back in Missouri, with the help of some antislavery lawyers, Scott and his wife Harriet Robinson sued for their freedom in the Missouri state courts. They argued that, because they had lived in a free state and a free territory, they should be free.

The Scotts lost their first trial but were able to win a second trial. Then Dred Scott's owners appealed, and over the next 11 years, their case went from the Missouri courthouse in Saint Louis to the Missouri Supreme Court, then on to federal courts, and finally all the way to the highest judicial body in the United States, the Supreme Court in Washington, D.C. The justices issued their decision in March of 1857. Seven of the nine judges wrote that, in their opinion, Dred Scott had not been set free by his owners. This meant not only that Scott had to return to slavery, but that as a slave, he was personal property and did not have the right to sue in a federal court.

The decision had broad implications across the United States. The Missouri Compromise of 1820 had forbidden slavery in the new American territories north of Missouri's southern border, but in the Dred Scott decision, this was declared unconstitutional. The justices said that Congress did not have the authority to forbid slavery in the newly acquired territories of the United States. This was a clear victory for the slave owners in the South. The court's decision fueled the growing antagonism between the free and slave states and contributed to the start of the American Civil War in 1861.

Chapter 3:
Listening: Taking Notes from a Lecture

As you listen to lectures on the TOEFL, you should take notes. Make sure that you:

- Write down key words, names, numbers, dates, or anything else you think is important
- Listen for strong general statements by the speaker, because they may be topic sentences or concluding sentences for paragraphs

The notes that you take as you are listening are very important, because they will help you answer questions such as:

- What is the main idea of the lecture?
- What is the purpose of this lecture: to inform, to persuade, to evaluate, to recommend?
- What are the important details in this lecture?

Outlining

If you just completed the writing chapter, you should be familiar with outlining. Remember, an outline is a skeletal structure of a text. It contains the main and supporting ideas in the order they are presented, but it does not necessarily include any specific details. Usually, an outline does not contain full sentences. Each subsection is listed in order using Roman numerals, and supporting ideas will be listed under each subsection using letters or numerals.

If you create an outline as you listen to a conversation or lecture on the TOEFL, you will have a more structured set of notes that you can then use to answer questions. Have a friend read the following transcribed lecture to you.

🔊 **Listening, Note-Taking Practice—Lecture Transcript**

Narrator: Listen to part of a talk in a history class.

Professor (female): Yesterday, we were discussing some of the economic and political ramifications of the Great Depression, the period that followed the infamous 1929 stock market crash, when social, political, and economic factors spurred almost 1,000 bank failures in a 12-month period.

Today we're going to talk about some of the social peculiarities of the same time period, the early 1930s. We'll look at the rise of bank robberies in the '30s and how it was possible for high-profile criminals to bend and shape the American public's opinion of the government and corporate institutions.

So, we've already talked about how the financial crises of the '30s had a negative impact on investor confidence. Whether or not it was true, many Americans felt that mismanagement of funds on the part of financial institutions was the cause of the Great Depression, and, as a result, was the cause of all their misery and hardship. This animosity toward financial institutions created an opportunity for some of the most notorious bank robbers in American history to win over the public. I'm sure you're already familiar with some of these names . . . John Dillinger, Harry Pierpont, Baby Face Nelson, and Bonnie and Clyde. This, uh, animosity toward banks and big business also gave the public a scapegoat for many of the things that were going wrong with the nation at the time.

What sets these criminals apart from their predecessors is that they somehow managed to win the admire, I mean admiration, of the public while stealing their money. Think about it for a minute. . . while the U.S. public should have been outraged that these criminals were able to walk into a bank, pull a gun on a teller, and walk out with a pile of cash—instead, they turned the thieves into celebrities and then gobbled up the news of their latest daring adventures. Frustrated by bank failures, rampant unemployment, and generally poor economic conditions, many citizens felt that these bank robbers were, were "getting back at" the banks—there was almost a sort of Robin Hood mentality—robbing the banks that robbed the public.

The most infamous of the outlaws was a guy named John Dillinger, a petty criminal who turned to robbing banks after spending eight and a half years in jail for attempting to hold up a grocery store. That's right. He didn't even rob the store. Dillinger confessed in court and was handed an extremely harsh sentence in relation to the crime he had planned to commit. During the time he spent in jail, he made friends with his fellow inmates and eventually hatched a plan to help them all escape from jail as soon as he was freed. It worked. Dillinger and his cohorts, who became known as the Dillinger Gang, then executed several bank robberies during 1933 and 1934.

Dillinger's exploits became so famous that they not only drew the attention of the media and the American public—who treated him like a celebrity—they eventually caught the attention of J. Edgar Hoover. In 1933, Hoover was the head of a brand-new government agency called the Federal Bureau of Investigation. Sound familiar? At this point, the public pretty much thought Hoover and the FBI were a joke, and the FBI's attempts to catch Dillinger did nothing to change public opinion at first. But Hoover was determined to catch Dillinger—not only to stop him from robbing banks, but also—and maybe more importantly for Hoover—to earn respect for the FBI.

As the months passed, Dillinger enraged Hoover so much that Hoover began calling him "Public Enemy

Number One" and made it his mission to apprehend Dillinger. In reality, Dillinger's ability to slip through the FBI's fingers at every turn made the FBI look inept and unprofessional, which just added to the public's infatuation with Dillinger, and stoked mistrust of the government's new law enforcement agency. Over a month-long period in 1935, I'm sorry, it was 1934—in one month in 1934, Dillinger managed to slip through the FBI's fingers four or five times—and every time he escaped, the public just fell more and more in love with him. It's amazing, isn't it? I mean, this guy walks into a bank, steals their savings, and every once in a while, he shoots and kills someone who gets in his way . . . and the public just eats it up. They treat him like a hero. They're sitting in movie theatres, watching the news, and they applaud him when accounts of his latest robbery show up on the screen.

Anyway, eventually, Hoover and his team captured most of Dillinger's gang and then finally cornered and killed Dillinger in July of 1934, after receiving a tip from his girlfriend. So what had been a fiasco for the FBI turned into their greatest success—after several thwarted efforts, the FBI got their man—and the credibility Hoover was hoping for.

Here is an example of the beginning of an outline based on the transcribed lecture. See if you can finish the outline by yourself.

I. The Great Depression of the 1930s
II. Social peculiarities
   A. Bank robberies
   B. High-profile criminals shaping public opinion
       1. Government
       2. Corporations

Notes

Outlining is important, but to do your best on the TOEFL Listening section, it's critical to understand the types of questions you will have to answer. Keep reading to learn more.

PRACTICE: LISTENING QUESTIONS

There are several different question types on the Listening section of the TOEFL. This chapter will cover two of these question types:

1. Understanding rhetorical function

2. Drawing an inference

Question Type 1: Understanding Rhetorical Function

There are two or three conversations and four to six lectures in the Listening section of the TOEFL.

One type of question that you will find on lectures—but generally not on conversations—in the Listening section of the TOEFL asks about rhetorical function. You have already studied one type of rhetorical function question in Chapter 1 in the Reading section. This type of question asks you to determine the speaker's intent—for example, is the speaker defining, describing, exemplifying, explaining, or doing something else? To answer this type of question correctly, you will need to be able to recognize the rhetorical devices used to achieve various rhetorical functions as well as other context and intonation cues.

Rhetorical Function Question Forms

There are four different forms of the rhetorical function question type in the Listening section. Two forms are the same as those in the Reading section—there is simply a question and four answer choices. In the first form, the question presents a rhetorical device and asks its function. In the second form, the question asks what a speaker does to achieve a given rhetorical function.

Following is an example of the second form. Notice that the function is presented in the question and you must determine how it is achieved. Remember that the question and the four answer choices in listening questions appear on the computer screen, but only the question is spoken by the narrator.

How does the professor support his statement that animosity toward financial institutions "created an opportunity for some of the most notorious bank robbers in American history to win over the public"?

(A) With an anecdote about ways the public expressed their anger and frustration

(B) With an explanation of the financial crises of the '30s

(C) With a list of bank robbers of the time who are still famous

(D) With a description of a known criminal

Answer: Choice (C) is correct. In the lecture, the professor follows the statement about robbers made famous because of animosity toward financial institutions by listing some criminals who are still famous today. Choice (B) mentions a topic that the professor spoke about in an earlier class. Choices (A) and (D) are also unrelated to this particular topic sentence, even though the idea of "anger and frustration" or "known criminal" seem to be key words that fit with "animosity" or "notorious."

In the third form of a rhetorical function question in the Listening section, you will hear an excerpt from the lecture, then the question will present a rhetorical device and ask you to determine its function.

Following is the transcript of a rhetorical function question, including an excerpt from the lecture "Cops and Robbers." On the actual test, you will only hear the excerpt—you will not be able to read it. Remember also that the question and the four answer choices in listening questions appear on the computer screen, but only the question is spoken by the narrator.

Narrator: Listen again to part of the lecture. Then answer the question.

Professor: In 1933, Hoover was the head of a brand-new government agency called the Federal Bureau of Investigation. Sound familiar? At this point, the public pretty much thought Hoover and the FBI were a joke, and the FBI's attempts to catch Dillinger did nothing to change public opinion at first.

Why does the professor say this: "In 1933, Hoover was the head of a brand-new government agency called the Federal Bureau of Investigation. Sound familiar?"

- (A) To ask students if they have heard of the Federal Bureau of Investigation
- (B) To elicit an answer from the students
- (C) To introduce students to the term *Federal Bureau of Investigation*
- (D) To engage the students

Answer: The professor's question in this excerpt does not seek an answer. It is merely a hook that speakers use to attract interest and signal the announcement of an impressive, surprising, or shocking statement. Choice (A) tries to distract you with a more literal and specific definition of "Sound familiar?" However, if taken as a literal question, it would lead the lecture off topic. Choice (B) tries to distract you by inferring that the professor is looking for an answer, as is normally the case for a question. Choice (C) tries to distract you by including the professor's words in the answer. Choice (D) best expresses the rhetorical function of the speaker's words in this case.

The fourth form of a rhetorical function question in the Listening section also presents a short excerpt from the lecture and asks what the rhetorical function of the entire excerpt is.

Following is the transcript of another rhetorical function question, including an excerpt from the lecture on "Cops and Robbers." Remember that you will not see the transcript on the test.

> Why does the professor say this: "Over a month-long period in 1935, I'm sorry, it was 1934—in one month in 1934, Dillinger managed to slip through the FBI's fingers four or five times—and every time he escaped, the public just fell more and more in love with him. It's amazing, isn't it?"
>
> (A) To elaborate an important point
>
> (B) To describe the difficulty the FBI experienced
>
> (C) To show a contrast with something said earlier
>
> (D) To elicit an answer from the students

Answer: The fact that the public saw Dillinger as a hero is an important point in the lecture, and in this quote, the professor elaborates this point. Therefore, (A) is correct.

Question Type 2: Drawing an Inference

There are two or three conversations and four to six lectures in the Listening section of the TOEFL.

Idiomatic expressions are words or phrases in which the literal meaning of each word does not necessarily help you understand the meaning of the words together. In other words, you have to make an inference about the meaning. Look at the following examples:

- John really looks blue today.
- John is looking a bit green.

Neither sentence is saying that John's skin is blue- or green-colored. Which sentence means that John looks sad? Which means that John looks sick?

You will probably encounter one question, sometimes two, on the lectures—but generally not on the conversations—in the Listening section of the TOEFL that tests your ability to infer meaning from context. You can often guess at the meaning of an idiomatic expression by looking at the parts of the sentence that you do understand.

Following are the transcripts of these types of questions. Read the examples and choose your answers. Remember that you will not see the narrator's introduction or the transcript of the excerpt on the test.

Narrator: Listen again to part of the lecture. Then answer the question.

Professor: At this point, the public pretty much thought Hoover and the FBI were a joke, and the FBI's attempts to catch Dillinger did nothing to change public opinion at first.

Why does the professor say this: " . . . the public pretty much thought Hoover and the FBI were a joke . . ."?

(A) The public thought that Hoover and the FBI were funny.

(B) People felt that Hoover and the FBI couldn't be taken seriously.

(C) People were unsure about the future of Hoover and the FBI.

(D) The FBI was soon going to become a very effective organization.

Answer: Choice (A) tries to distract you by playing off the literal meaning of *joke* as a something that is humorous or funny. Choice (C) is too vague. In choice (D), the word *effective* has a positive connotation for producing good results. The lecture is not emphasizing the future of the FBI. Choice (B) provides the correct answer, explaining that when the public watched the FBI fail to catch Dillinger, it felt that the FBI was not really a powerful law enforcement organization.

Narrator: Listen again to part of the lecture. Then answer the question.

Professor: In reality, Dillinger's ability to slip through the FBI's fingers at every turn made the FBI look inept and unprofessional, which just added to the public's infatuation with Dillinger and stoked mistrust of the government's new law enforcement agency.

Why does the professor say this: ". . . made the FBI look inept and unprofessional, which just added to the public's infatuation with Dillinger and stoked mistrust of the government's new law enforcement agency"?

- (A) The repeated escapes added to the public's negative opinion of the FBI.
- (B) The repeated escapes created mistrust of the FBI.
- (C) The repeated escapes improved the way the public viewed the FBI.
- (D) The repeated escapes angered the public.

Answer: The correct answer is (A). The word *stoked* is used idiomatically by the professor, meaning "to make something burn hotter or faster," in this case public mistrust of the FBI. Can you see how the three distracter answer choices might appear correct if you didn't know the idiomatic use of *stoke*?

When you're ready, move on to the next chapter.

Chapter 4:
Speaking: Describing from Experience and Summarizing a Lecture

Two of the speaking tasks that are covered in this chapter include:

1. Describing something from your own experience

2. Summarizing a lecture

First, here is a review of content and function words.

Content and Function Words

Whether a word in a sentence is stressed or unstressed in spoken English depends on several factors. One factor is the importance of the meaning of a word to the phrase or sentence in which it appears. Which words or phrases do you think are the most important for the meaning of the following sentence?

> The Dred Scott decision of 1857 was a milestone in United States history.

The words that carry more meaning are in **bold** in the sentence that follows. The other words contribute less to the overall meaning of the sentence, though they convey grammatical meaning.

> The **Dred Scott decision** of 1857 was a **milestone** in **United States history.**

The words that carry the meaning of a sentence are called *content words*. Content words are often nouns, adjectives, verbs, and adverbs. The words that convey grammatical meaning are called *function words*. Articles, conjunctions, and prepositions are often function words. A tendency in spoken English is to stress many of the content words. The function words generally remain unstressed, but this depends on the context and message being conveyed.

PRACTICE: SPEAKING TASKS

Task 1: Describing Something from Your Own Experience

There are six tasks in the Speaking section of the TOEFL.

The first requires you to speak for 45 seconds about a topic based on personal experience. You will be asked to describe or explain something about yourself, your family, your country, or some similar topic. For example, you may be asked to describe a popular sport in your country. Before you start thinking about a popular sport in your own country, take a moment to think of and write down questions you would like to ask someone else about sport in their home country. Don't just think about how the sport is played. You could also ask about its history, where it is played, and who plays it.

Now practice the following TOEFL question for speaking task 1. Ask a friend or another student to read the narrator prompt and question to you, then listen to your response. Remember that you will not see the narrator's introduction to the question on the test but you will both hear and read the question.

🔘 Speaking, Task 1

Narrator: In this question, you will be asked to talk about a familiar topic. After you hear the question, you will have 15 seconds to prepare your response and 45 seconds to speak.

> Describe a popular sport or game in your native country. Explain how it is played and why it is important to people in your country. Include details and examples.
>
> 15 seconds to prepare   45 seconds to speak

Notes

Evaluate yourself using the following criteria:

Criteria	Comments	Action to Improve
Clarity and pronunciation		
Organization		
Details and examples		
Grammar and vocabulary		

Task 6: Summarizing a Lecture

There are six tasks in the Speaking section of the TOEFL. The sixth requires you to speak for 60 seconds, giving a summary of a short academic lecture. As you listen, you should take notes on the main idea and important points. Then you will present your summary.

When taking notes:

- Identify what kind of lecture it is: descriptive, cause and effect, informative, narrative, etc.
- Identify key parts by listening for stressed words and phrases

- Note key pieces of information such as names, dates, and places
- Identify how the lecture is organized: What are the main points, and what are examples?

When summarizing:

- Present the main idea of the lecture
- Paraphrase some of the examples and details

Practice the following TOEFL question. Following, you will find the transcript for Speaking Task 6. Ask a friend or another student to read the transcript of the short lecture to you as well as the following prompt. As you listen, take notes, and then summarize the main points using the strategies previously mentioned. Remember that you will not see the narrator's introduction to the question on the test, and you will both hear and read the question. Now listen to the introduction and question.

● Speaking, Task 6 Lecture

Narrator: Task 6. For this task, you will hear a short academic talk. You will hear a question about it. You will then have 20 seconds to prepare your response and 60 seconds to speak.

Narrator: Listen to part of a talk in an urban history class.

Professor: Usually, when people talk about the Harlem Renaissance—the period extending from the end of World War I to the Great Depression in the mid-1930s—they focus on the cultural aspects, and particularly on the great black writers of the period who produced an extensive body of literature of all types: drama, poetry, fiction, and nonfiction.

Certainly, culture was an important part of the rebirth of this New York neighborhood. But there's another element of the Harlem Renaissance that can't be ignored, and without which this rebirth would never have come about, and that is the economic aspect. Blacks began settling in the northern cities of the United States soon after the end of the Civil War. This migration to the north was the result of a variety of factors. Blacks were eager to escape the racism and discrimination they suffered in the South. At the same time, with the South in the midst of an economic depression, blacks saw the North as the land of opportunity.

Before it became the social and cultural center of black America, Harlem was a white, upper-class neighborhood inhabited by a large number of Jews and Italians. Thanks in large part to huge improvements in public transportation—the advent of the bus and the elevated train—Harlem enjoyed a real estate boom, which spurred a big surge in construction. Then, suddenly, between 1903 and 1905, an economic crisis brought a sudden end to the construction, leaving many homes and apartment buildings abandoned and unfinished. At about this same time, the subway line that connected Harlem to downtown Manhattan was completed. The existence of convenient public transportation and the availability of affordable housing were two factors that paved the way for blacks to move into Harlem in large numbers.

Ⓜ **Speaking, Task 6 Prompt**

Using points and examples from the talk, explain how economic factors contributed to the Harlem Renaissance in New York City in the early 1900s.

| 20 seconds to prepare | 60 seconds to speak |

Evaluate yourself using the following criteria:

Criteria	Comments	Action to Improve
Clarity and pronunciation		
Organization		
Details and examples		
Grammar and vocabulary		

Now have a friend read the following sample response. How is it different from yours? How is it similar?

Speaking: Task 6 Sample Response

The speaker describes how Harlem became a social and cultural center for black culture in the United States. Harlem used to be populated by white, upper-class people, mostly Jewish and Italian. There was a real estate boom early in the 20th century, but that ended, and there were a lot of empty homes and apartment buildings. Because a subway line that went to Harlem had just been finished and the living costs were so low, many blacks coming from the South found that Harlem was a convenient and affordable place to live.

Once so many Blacks had moved to the area, the growing culture led to the Harlem Renaissance, which produced many famous musicians, writers, and other artists.

Congratulations! You have finished your first set of reading, writing, listening, and speaking skills. When you are ready, turn to Part 2 to learn more skills and strategies for mastering the TOEFL.

Part Three
Building on the Basics

Part Three builds upon the basic skills and strategies
that you learned in the first set of chapters in Part Two.
Be sure that you complete all of the practice exercises
and sample questions.

Chapter 5:
Reading: The Main Idea

Details in a Reading Passage

The first paragraph or first few sentences of a news report is called the lead. The lead generally answers all or most of the main questions a reporter must answer:

- Who?
- Where?
- What?
- When?
- Why?
- How?

Imagine how difficult it would be to understand a story in the news if these six questions weren't answered. That's because the answers to all six of these questions provide important details that together express the main idea of a news story. In this way, the lead to a news report is a concentration of the most important details in a passage, and it is an excellent example of how details combine to express the main idea.

Although none of the reading passages on the TOEFL is a news report, you will have to understand details in TOEFL reading passages—essentially, answers to the previous six questions—and how those details combine to express the main idea of the passage. The following reading practice will show you how details are presented in a news report and how details combine to express the main idea.

Let's look at an example of detail identification. First, read the following passage.

The History of American Comics

Comic books, graphic novels, and the Sunday comics can all trace their heritage back to book illustrations, which have been around as long as the printed word. But cartoons and comics have always been more than simple drawings, and the characters and stories they tell often reflect on the society that created them. The first editorial cartoon published in the United States was drawn by Benjamin Franklin in 1754. An illustration of a snake with a severed head with the words "Join or Die" printed below it, the cartoon was intended to convince the American colonies to join together and form the United States.

At that time, however, the comic book as we now know it had not yet evolved. In 1895, an artist named Richard Outcault created what is often referred to as the first comic strip, called *The Yellow Kid*. The distinguishing feature of Outcault's new strip was his use of the speech balloon, an outlined shape or bubble within the picture frame that contained the words that the characters spoke. *The Yellow Kid* first appeared in newspapers in New York City, where Outcault drew pictures for Joseph Pulitzer and William Randolph Hearst, two of the most famous newspaper owners in the history of the United States.

Aside from being a publishing success, *The Yellow Kid* was so popular that it was heavily marketed in the New York area, with the huge-eared main character, Mickey Dugan, appearing on packs of chewing gum, postcards, baby clothes, and even home appliances. Because *The Yellow Kid* comic strip appeared in newspapers that were better known for sensational headlines and scandalous stories than for accuracy and factual reporting, this style of gaudy, opinionated news reporting became known as "yellow journalism," a term still in use today to describe news reporting that is overly sensational or biased.

The first comic book to be published in the form we are familiar with today was called *Funnies on Parade*. In 1933, M.C. Gaines and Harry Wildenberg convinced the printing company they worked for, Eastern Color Printing, to print 10,000 copies of a small collection of comic strips gathered from newspapers. Procter and Gamble then gave away these comic books as part of a sales promotion. The giveaways were so popular that Eastern Color decided to print the first regularly published comic book, *Famous Funnies*, in 1934. The fact that the contents of these books were often humorous led people to call them "funnies" or "comic" books.

In the later part of the 1930s, war was looming on the horizon, and American funnies stopped being funny. Instead of collections of light-hearted short strips, comic book companies began to publish comics that relied heavily on detective fiction and adventure stories. The strong, sure-of-heart protagonists were reassuring to readers who were faced with the growing likelihood of a global war, and so comics became even more action-packed, heroes became even faster and more powerful, and villains were more sinister. Then, in 1938, the world of comic books changed forever: the superhero was born. Superheroes were an entirely new idea to the American public, and people quickly fell in love with the brightly costumed crime fighters with their superhuman powers and meek, mild-mannered alter egos. Soon stores couldn't keep comic books on their shelves. The idea was such a success that within two years, almost every comic book company was publishing at least one superhero comic.

With the invention of the superhero, comic books thrived in the 1930s and '40s. After World War II, new genres of comic books appeared, including teen humor, science fiction, and romance comics. But the success did not last. Comic books became so popular that the United

States Senate Subcommittee on Juvenile Delinquency began to investigate the role of comic books in poor grades and juvenile crime. As a result, some communities around the United States even passed laws banning comic books entirely. Sales of comic books declined sharply, and over the next decade, the superhero genre was almost completely wiped out.

During the 1970s, the Cold War dominated people's lives. Many were growing tired of living with the constant threat of nuclear conflict between the United States and the Soviet Union. The few comic book companies who survived the business drought of the 1950s and '60s desperately needed a boost to keep from going bankrupt. And so comics changed again to match American society. The new comics were much darker than those of the 1940s. They often dealt with real life issues, and their main characters were not always superpowered crime fighters. Instead they were often torn by the same conflicts and problems that their readers dealt with in everyday life. Readers found that they could identify with these new, flawed heroes, and as a result, they began to read comics again. While the industry is nowhere near as successful as it was in the Golden Age of the 1930s and '40s, the comic book has recovered much of its popularity.

Now look at the following lead sentences from the passage:

Comic books, graphic novels, and the Sunday comics can all trace their heritage back to book illustrations, which have been around as long as the printed word. But cartoons and comics have always been more than simple drawings, and the characters and stories they tell often reflect on the society that created them.

Which of the following questions can be answered by the information presented in the lead?

- Who?
- What?
- When?
- Where?
- Why?
- How?

Look at the entire passage again and find details to answer the previous questions more completely. An example has been done for you.

Who?	What?	When?	Where?	Why?	How?
Comic books	Changed with American society	Beginning in 1754	In the United States	People needed characters that were related to the time	Superheroes evolved to reassure people before World War II, and flawed, realistic heroes evolved to address the anxiety of the Cold War

Transitions

Transitional words and phrases help you move from one idea to the next. This is important in a news report, because journalists must convey many ideas in a short passage. It is also important in academic passages, such as those on the TOEFL, which present a good deal of information in a short space.

One way to transition effectively is to repeat or to use synonyms for the key words or phrases. For example, in the sentences from the previous text, the journalist uses the synonym *drawings* to transition from the word *illustrations* in the previous sentence.

> Comic books, graphic novels, and the Sunday comics can all trace their heritage back to book **illustrations,** which have been around as long as the printed word. But cartoons and comics have always been more than simple **drawings.**

Skimming

Remember from Chapter 1 about reading that skimming a passage is the best way to determine its main idea and important points as well as what type of text it is. To skim a passage, pass your eyes quickly over the text (maybe in as few as 15–20 seconds), not really reading but trying to notice the important parts. In this way, you get a general overview of the passage. In Chapter 1, you also learned that when you skim you should try to:

- Identify the thesis statement and topic sentences
- Recognize the basic organization
- Note repeated key words

Consider the following passage on meteorites. The paragraphs have been numbered for your convenience in answering the subsequent questions that refer back to specific parts of the passage.

Meteorites

(1) Have you ever seen a shooting star? Did you make a wish? Known as meteors, these brief, bright streaks of light in the night sky have been a source of wonder for ages. In fact, Chinese astronomers were carefully observing and recording the appearance of meteors as early as 687 B.C.E. A meteor is a chunk of material that is pulled into our atmosphere by Earth's gravitational field. Traveling at tens of thousands of miles an hour, the meteor is heated until it glows by the friction caused when it enters our atmosphere, creating the incandescent trail we see from the ground. It is estimated that between 1,000 and 10,000 tons of matter fall into Earth's atmosphere every day. The vast majority of this material is made up of tiny, dust-sized grains that fall gently to Earth because they are too small to burn in the atmosphere. However, approximately 500 baseball-sized rocks reach the Earth's surface every year.

(2) A meteor that has not yet made contact with the atmosphere is called a meteoroid, while a meteor that falls all the way to the ground is called a meteorite. Meteorites can be

divided into five different categories: iron, stony-iron, and the three subtypes of stony meteorites.

(3)   Iron meteorites are mostly made of the metals nickel and iron. These meteorites are not very common, making up about 6 percent of all meteors that fall to Earth. Several current theories speculate that iron meteorites are fragments from the outer cores of former planets or asteroids that broke up long ago. Native American tribes found an excellent example of an iron meteorite in what is now the southwestern part of the United States. For centuries, they collected parts of the Canyon Diablo meteorite, which is estimated to have been about 150 feet wide and weighed 63,000 tons. When the meteorite hit, it was traveling nearly 40,000 miles an hour, creating a crater nearly a mile wide and about 600 feet deep. Although the impact occurred nearly 50,000 years ago, Meteor Crater, as it is now known, is still clearly visible and is a tourist attraction in Arizona.

(4)   Stony-iron meteorites compose less than 2 percent of all meteorites that land on our planet. Partly metal, they are made of an iron-nickel alloy mixed with other nonmetallic mineral matter, believed to be similar to the material that exists where the Earth's core meets the mantle, or outer layer. A stony-iron meteorite was found in Huckitta, Australia, in 1924. Thousands of pieces of the shattered meteorite were found over the next few decades. The largest piece weighed more than one and a half tons. A large cut section of this meteorite can be found in the American Museum of Natural History in New York.

(5)   The last group is the stony meteorites, which can be divided into three separate subtypes. The first is the chondrites, which are the most commonly found meteorite, making up around 86 percent of all meteorites that fall to Earth. They can be identified by chondrules, tiny blobs of formerly melted mineral that have joined with other minerals to form solid rock. Typically, chondrules are very small, with an average diam-

eter of one millimeter. Scientists believe that chondrites are among the oldest rocks in our solar system, and that they are similar to the outermost layers of Earth.

(6)   Carbonaceous chondrites, another type of stony meteorite, are very rare. They contain the element carbon, an essential component of life on Earth. One of the most famous examples of this type of meteorite fell to Earth in Murchison, Australia, in 1969. When scientists examined the Murchison stone, they were amazed to find that it contained several different amino acids, organic compounds that make life as we know it possible. This discovery confirmed that there is still a lot we do not fully understand about meteorites and their formation. In particular, some researchers claimed that the Murchison meteorite and others like it were evidence that life on Earth did not begin here but was brought from somewhere else by a carbonaceous chondrite meteorite.

(7)   The last group of stony meteorites is the achondrites, which make up just over 7 percent of all meteorites that fall to earth. These are made of stone as well but do not have chondrules. These meteorites may have the most interesting story of all, because scientists believe that some of the achondrites that have been found were once part of Mars and our own moon.

1. How does the passage seem to be organized—by time, process, or category?

   _____

2. Make a list of words that are frequently repeated throughout the text.

   _____

   _____

   _____

   _____

   _____

Next, using the information gathered from skimming, see how well you can answer the following questions.

3. Which of the following best expresses the main idea of the passage?

   A. Meteors fall all around the world.

   B. Iron, stony-iron, and stony are a few types of meteorites.

   C. Chondrites are the oldest rocks in our solar system.

   D. Meteorites provide interesting clues about our solar system.

4. According to the passage, a chondrule

   A. is the same as a piece of stone.

   B. can only be found in Australia.

   C. exemplifies mineral formations in meteors.

   D. characterizes the most common type of meteorite.

5. Skim the passage one more time and choose one of the text types that you think best describes it. Explain your choice.

   A. Descriptive

   B. Compare/contrast

   C. Explanation of a process

   D. Definition with examples

Answers:

1. The passage is organized by category: iron, stony-iron, and stony meteorites.

2. Meteor, meteorite, fall, iron, nickel, stone, chondrites

3. (B) Iron, stony-iron, and stony are a few types of meteorites.

4. (D) characterizes the most common type of meteorite.

5. (D) Definition with examples. The passage defines meteorites and provides five examples.

Outlining

Remember from Chapter 2 on writing that, when outlining, you must first determine the main ideas and supporting information, then organize this material in a logical manner. In this way, an outline clearly shows the relationship between the main idea, most important points, and supporting details. Here is an example of an outline of the first two paragraphs of the text on meteorites.

I. Definition of meteorites
   A. Facts
      1. Observed by Chinese astronomers in 687 B.C.E.
      2. Chunk of space material
      3. Pulled into Earth's atmosphere by gravity
      4. Very high speeds + friction from atmosphere—burning trail
      5. 1,000 to 10,000 tons of material fall on Earth every day
      6. ~500 baseball-sized meteorites land each year
   B. Terms
      1. Meteoroid—falling object that has not hit the ground
      2. Meteorite—object that fell all the way to the ground
   C. Five types
      1. Iron
      2. Stony-iron
      3. Stony (three subtypes)

Now, try taking notes yourself on paragraph three of the passage on iron meteorites.

Notes

Identifying Examples

Several transitional words or phrases can be used to give an example in writing. Some of these phrases are:

- *for example*
- *for instance*
- *in other words*
- *in particular*
- *namely*
- *specifically*
- *such as*
- *thus*
- *to illustrate*

Different types of examples can be used to illustrate a point in writing. Some of these types include:

- Statistics or equations
- Details that represent the main topic
- Anecdote, description, or situation that explains the idea

Look at the following sentences from the text "Meteorites." What types of examples are they? The first example has been done for you.

1. Known as meteors, these brief, bright streaks of light in the night sky have been a source of wonder for ages. In fact, Chinese astronomers were carefully observing and recording the appearance of meteors as early as 687 B.C.E.

Type of example: Details that represent the main topic

2. Native American tribes found an excellent example of an iron meteorite in what is now the southwestern part of the United States. For centuries, they collected parts of the Canyon Diablo meteorite, which is estimated to have been about 150 feet wide and weighed 63,000 tons.

Type of example: _____

3. The first type is the chondrites, which are the most commonly found meteorite, making up around 86 percent of all meteorites that fall to Earth.

Type of example: _____

4. This confirmed that there is still a lot we do not fully understand about meteorites and their formation. In particular, some researchers claimed that the Murchison meteorite and others like it were evidence that life on Earth did not begin here but was brought from somewhere else by a carbonaceous chondrite meteorite.

Type of example: _____

Answers:

1. Type of example: Details that represent the main topic

2. Type of example: Details that represent the main topic

3. Type of example: Statistics or equations

4. Type of example: Situation that explains the idea

PRACTICE: READING QUESTIONS

Understanding the question types is important for knowing how and where you can apply your strategies. There are several question types on the Reading section of the TOEFL. In Chapter 1, we covered three types:

1. Drawing an inference

2. Summarizing the most important points

3. Understanding rhetorical function

This chapter will cover two more types:

1. Understanding details

2. Understanding details as they relate to the main idea (schematic table)

It is important to understand what each of these question types is testing, as well as how the types are presented. To learn more, keep reading.

Question Type 4: Understanding Details

There are three to five passages in the Reading section of the TOEFL, each of which is followed by three to eight understanding details questions.

One type of question on the TOEFL requires you to answer questions about details found in a reading passage. To answer this type of question correctly, you will need to use several of the strategies you have been practicing:

- Skimming the passage for main ideas and important points
- Taking effective notes that summarize the main ideas and important points

On the TOEFL, you will need to be able to identify the key words in both questions and answer choices, and you will need to skim the passage for those same words or their synonyms. For example, the question here, about "Meteorites," has key words that have been underlined.

> According to the passage, the <u>metals</u> that <u>constitute</u> the most common <u>meteorites</u> are . . . .

From your skimming and outlining, you might already remember that *meteorites* and *metals* are words that are used frequently in the passage. If not, you can skim the passage quickly to find them. By skimming, you can also find a synonym for the key word *constitute*; it is *to be made of*, found in paragraph four.

Now look at the question and two answer choices, and answer the questions that follow.

According to the passage, the <u>metals</u> that <u>constitute</u> the most common <u>meteorites</u> are . . .

(A) nickel and iron combined into an alloy with other materials.

(B) matter similar to the boundary between the Earth's mantle and core.

---

1. What are the key words in the answer choices?

   _____

   _____

2. Which key words in the answer choices are repeated in paragraph four?

   _____

   _____

3. Which key words in the answer choices have synonyms in paragraph four?

   _____

   _____

4. Based on your answers to the previous questions, is (A) or (B) a better answer choice?

   _____

   _____

Answers:

1. Nickel, iron, alloy, materials, combined, boundary, between, matter, mantle, core

2. Nickel, iron, alloy, materials, matter, Earth, mantle, core

3. Combined (mixed)

4. (A) is a better choice, because it talks about the metals iron and nickel being mixed, while (B) only refers to nonspecific matter

Using the skill of skimming and looking back at the notes you have taken on paragraphs one, two, and three, answer the questions that follow.

All of the following are mentioned in paragraph one as characteristics of a meteor EXCEPT that

(A) it is pulled into Earth's atmosphere by gravity.

(B) it creates its own heat as it enters the atmosphere.

(C) it travels at tens of thousands of miles an hour.

(D) it creates a bright glowing trail as it descends.

Answer: The correct answer is (B) because, according to the reading, a meteor gets hot because of the friction of the Earth's atmosphere. Therefore, the meteor is not creating its own heat as it comes down… Choice (A) is not correct because this is actually a fact mentioned about meteors in the reading, whereas the question asks for something that is not a characteristic of a meteor. Choices (C) and (D) are both incorrect for the same reason as choice (A): they are mentioned as characteristics of meteors.

In deciding on the correct choice for detail questions, be aware of distracters that do any of the following:

- Use key words, phrases, or information from the passage in a way unrelated to the question
- Use key words or phrases from the passage but are untrue
- Express ideas that are not mentioned in the passage

Now read and answer the following *detail* questions.

According to the passage, meteoroids

(A) join with minerals to form solid rock.

(B) are made of crystalline minerals and dust.

(C) have not landed on Earth.

(D) cause friction when they are heated.

Answer: Choice (C) is correct because the passage mentions that a meteoroid has not hit Earth's atmosphere. (A) is incorrect because it uses key words from the passage but not correctly. Chondrules join with minerals to form rock, not meteoroids. Choice (B) uses words or phrases from the passage, but it is an untrue statement. The passage states that meteors are made of iron, nickel, and minerals, not crystalline minerals and dust. Choice (D) also uses key words, but is an untrue statement; meteoroids do not cause friction when they are heated.

How do scientists think that iron meteorites formed?

(A) They burned in the Earth's atmosphere.

(B) They were probably created by comets.

(C) They used to be segments of meteoroids.

(D) They were likely fragments of the outer cores of former planets.

Answer: The correct answer is (D). Look at the distracter answer choices and determine how they are written to distract you.

Question Type 5: Understanding Details as They Relate to the Main Idea (Schematic Table)

There are three to five passages in the Reading section of the TOEFL, one of which may be followed by one question in schematic table format.

This type of question has a schematic table format that asks you to select several appropriate phrases from a list and match them to a related category. To answer this question, you must understand how particular supporting details presented in the passage develop two or three important points in the passage. As with regular detail questions, to answer this type of question correctly, you will need to skim while using your notes to find the answers quickly in the passage.

Look at the answer choices and then answer the questions that follow.

Answer Choices	Chondrites
• Make up around 86 percent of all meteorites that fall to Earth	
• Can be identified by chondrules	
• Are among the oldest rocks in our solar system	
• Are very rare	
• Sometimes contain amino acids	**Carbonacious Chondrites**
• Might have contributed to the beginning of life on Earth	
• A famous example landed in Australia	
• An iron-copper alloy mixed with other non-metallic mineral matter	

1. Without looking at the text and based only on your memory from skimming the passage, write down in which paragraph you think each of the answer choices might be mentioned.

   _____

   _____

2. Identify the key words in each answer choice.

   _____

   _____

Now, using the skill of skimming, select the appropriate phrases from the answer choices. Match them to the type of stony meteorite to which they relate. TWO of the answer choices will NOT be used.

Here are the answer explanations.

The following answer choices belong in the box under the heading "Chondrites":

- Make up around 86 percent of all meteorites that fall to Earth
- Can be identified by chondrules
- Are among the oldest rocks in our solar system

The following answer choices belong in the box under the heading "Carbonaceous Chondrites":

- Are very rare
- Sometimes contain amino acids
- Might have contributed to the beginning of life on Earth
- A famous example landed in Australia

The answer choice

- An iron-copper alloy mixed with other nonmetallic mineral matter

is incorrect, because it includes information from the passage in a way unrelated to the question. This information is about stony meteorites, not iron or stony-iron meteorites.

The answer choice

- Contains the oldest examples of chondrules

is incorrect because it is untrue. In this case, chondrules are a shared characteristic of both types of meteorite, but the passage does not address the age of the meteorites.

Distracters

Now we'll review distracters in this question type. Two kinds of distracters to be aware of are distracters that do the following:

- Use key words, phrases, or information from the passage in a way unrelated to the question
- Use key words or phrases from the passage but are untrue

Read the following incorrect answers for the question about meteorites and write which type of distracter is used:

- Are the second most carbonaceous meteorite

———————————————————————

- Have chondrules and make up 6 percent of all meteorites

———————————————————————

- Do not always penetrate to the Earth's mantle upon impact

———————————————————————

- Commonly break up as they enter the atmosphere

———————————————————————

Answers:

- Are the second most carbonaceous meteorite. Uses key words or phrases from the passage but is untrue:
- Have chondrules and make up 6 percent of all meteorites. Uses key words or phrases from the passage but is untrue:
- Do not always penetrate to the Earth's mantle upon impact. Uses key words, phrases, or information from the passage in a way unrelated to the question:

- Commonly break up as they enter the atmosphere: Uses key words, phrases, or information from the passage in a way unrelated to the question.

Now that you have reviewed some reading strategies, let's move on to some writing strategies.

Chapter 6:
Writing: Responding to Reading and Listening

Writing an Essay in Response to a Reading Passage and a Lecture

When you take the TOEFL, you will write an essay in which you use information you have learned from both reading and listening sources. First, you will have three minutes to read a passage on an academic topic. You may take notes while you read. Then you will listen to and take notes on a lecture about the same topic. Information in the lecture will conflict somewhat with the information in the reading passage; that is, a different perspective on the topic will be presented.

You will have 20 minutes to write this essay. You may use the notes you took to help you write your essay. An effective essay will be 150–225 words long.

Make sure to read the prompt carefully to determine exactly what it is asking you to do. In your response, be prepared to do the following:

- Summarize information provided in the reading passage and the lecture
- Define a specific term or idea
- Provide examples from the reading passage and lecture

Planning a Definition Essay

While this first essay in the Writing section of the TOEFL cannot be categorized as a traditional essay type, it may have characteristics of a definition essay. The reading passage and the lecture essentially define the topic in different ways, and you must synthesize and summarize those definitions. You will not be asked to express your opinion. This chapter focuses on writing a definition essay, so that you can learn and then apply the relevant skills to writing the first essay on the TOEFL.

Before you begin writing a definition essay, you should always take a little time to plan. There are two things you should include in your planning:

1. The message and information you wish to communicate in the essay

2. A strategy for organizing that information

Here is a list of steps to follow to help you plan your essay and a description of each step.

1. **Identify the message or purpose of your essay.** The most important aspect of any essay you write is its purpose. This purpose must be communicated clearly to the reader. The best place to do this is in the introduction, and the most common device for doing so is called the thesis statement. Usually, the thesis statement is the last sentence of the introductory paragraph.

    Remember the discussion of the thesis statement in Chapter 2 on writing? If not, here's a brief review of thesis statements:

    A thesis statement can do two important things. First, the thesis statement can identify the writer's purpose in writing the essay: the message, lesson, or principal idea the writer wishes to communicate. Second, the thesis statement can give a clear indication of the organization of the essay by listing each of the topics to be discussed in the body of the essay and doing so in the same order that the reader will actually encounter them. This is called forecasting and is an important courtesy to your reader; a detailed thesis statement is like a map to the essay.

2. Identify two or three aspects of the main topic, as expressed in the reading passage and the lecture, that you will discuss in your essay. Each of them should be a subtopic of the essay's main idea. Once you know what they are, formulate each into a sentence. These will be your topic sentences and will introduce each of your body paragraphs.

3. Make a list of information that you can use to detail, exemplify, or support each of your topic sentences. You should have at least two or three pieces of information for each topic sentence. For the first task in the TOEFL Writing section, this information should come from what you have read and heard.

4. Draw an outline of the essay you are going to write. Preparing an outline ahead of time will give you a clear mental picture of your essay, allowing you to visualize each step you will follow as you write. Your outline does not need to be thoroughly detailed, but it should, at minimum, refer to the thesis, body topics, and supporting information you identified in steps 1 through 3.

Here is a model outline for a definition essay with supporting examples. (Of course, you do not need to have exactly three body paragraphs, with exactly two details per paragraph. This is a basic structure.)

I. Introductory paragraph
   A. Background information
   B. Thesis statement
II. First body paragraph
   A. First supporting detail
   B. Second supporting detail
III. Second body paragraph
   A. First supporting detail
   B. Second supporting detail
IV. Third body paragraph
   A. First supporting detail
   B. Second supporting detail
V. Conclusion

Note-Taking

Taking notes from reading and listening passages requires identifying the information which is critical to understanding the central ideas expressed and distinguishing this information from less critical material. Here is a list of strategies to help you do this more effectively:

- **Pay careful attention to the introduction of the reading passage and the lecture.** The introduction will usually tell you the writer's or speaker's purpose. It is essential for your summary to reflect that purpose.

- **The last sentence of the introduction is usually the thesis statement.** The thesis statement can do two things. First, it may indicate the feeling or opinion the author has about the topic, helping you to identify the purpose. But it may also list the key points that will be addressed. You can write these down; they will help you know what to look for or listen for later.

- **Use the topic sentences.** Topic sentences are another way of identifying key points and will also tell you when the writer or speaker is leaving one topic and moving to a new one. Your notes should reflect each of these topics.

- **Pay attention to examples.** Examples are carefully chosen to illustrate the topic and will help you and the readers of your summary to understand the points being discussed. If each example illustrates a contrast or difference, it will be useful to write each one down. However, if several examples illustrate a single subtopic, it is not necessary to write all of them. Choose the most important one or the one that is easiest for you to understand.

- **Numbers, dates, and statistics are carefully chosen for their importance and relevance.** They are also relatively easy to hear and quick to write down. Pay attention to them.

Now practice note taking. Read the following sample reading passage, "Global Warming," carefully and try to employ the note-taking strategies previously discussed.

Reading Passage: Global Warming

"Global warming" is defined as an increase in the Earth's atmospheric temperature. Causes of global warming can be categorized in two ways: human-induced warming and natural climate fluctuations that have been in place for thousands of years.

Many scientists believe that human activity has very little, if any, impact on the recent warming trend on Earth. These researchers point to the various ice ages in the earth's history, the most recent of which occurred 15,000 years ago, almost 14,000 years before industry and human habitation had any impact on the atmosphere. While not as well documented, these ice ages might have been tempered by warmer periods throughout history—meaning the current increase in the earth's atmospheric temperature is nothing more than a cyclical natural phenomenon.

In fact, it is difficult to determine the impact of humans on the environment, as we have only been documenting weather changes for the last hundred years. Most scientists agree that data from a longer time period is needed to build an accurate picture of temperature fluctuations. Over the past hundred years, the temperature has only risen marginally—about one degree. This warming has not been uniform, as some areas of the world have actually experienced cooling over the past 20 years, even with record activity caused by El Niño in 1997 and 1998.

In reality, there is no conclusive evidence that human activity has any effect on the Earth's surface temperature. While environmental activists and other alarmists are quick to blame increased carbon dioxide emissions for the recent trend, the truth is that nobody knows whether a similar warming—and cyclical cooling—occurred before the advent of temperature-related technology in the late 1900s.

Notes

Example of Notes Taken from the Reading Passage

I. Global warming
   A. Possible causes
      1. Human induced
      2. Natural climate fluctuations over thousands of years
II. Possible nonhuman causes
   A. Ice ages
      1. Most recent—15,000 years ago, before industry impact on atmosphere
      2. Ice ages may alternate with warmer periods
      3. Could be just a natural cycle
III. Limitations on evidence of human responsibility
   A. Recording limitations
      1. Weather has only been tracked for the last hundred years
      2. Scientists agree that more data is needed for accuracy
   B. Facts about temperature
      1. Global temperature has only risen about one degree over last hundred years
      2. Warming has not been uniform
      3. Some parts of the world have cooled (El Niño in 1997 and 1998)
IV. No conclusive evidence of effect of humanity on global temperature
   A. Environmental activists
      1. Alarmist
      2. Blame carbon dioxide emissions from human industry
   B. No one knows key facts
      1. Whether similar warming occurred before human industry
      2. Whether cyclical cooling occurred before human industry

You can apply the same principles to taking notes from a short lecture. Next is a transcript of a global warming lecture. Ask a friend or another student to read the transcript to you and take notes.

🔊 Note-Taking Practice—Lecture Transcript

Narrator: Listen to a professor in a biology class.

Professor (Male): Although scientists cannot predict future temperature trends with 100 percent accuracy, much evidence points to a global warming trend that may eventually make this planet uninhabitable. While there have been large variations in temperature on Earth for thousands of years, the current warming trend is cause for alarm—and we only have ourselves to blame for it.

This is because carbon dioxide—a gas that occurs naturally in the atmosphere—is now produced at alarming rates by industry. Carbon dioxide, or CO_2, is a "greenhouse gas," one of the gases that traps infrared radiation upon release into the atmosphere, making the Earth warm enough to support human life.

However, too much greenhouse gas in the atmosphere will cause a radical increase in the surface temperature of the Earth. And ever since the Industrial Revolution, the level of greenhouse gas released into the atmosphere has increased dramatically.

So as a result, the temperature of the Earth has risen by about one degree over the past century, with accelerated warming in the past two decades. Sure, CO_2 is released naturally into the atmosphere, but it's released at a much higher rate when humans burn solid waste, fossil fuels, and wood products. And this increase will accelerate the natural rate of climate change . . . scientists expect an increase of up to ten degrees in the next century.

Some people will try to explain away the global warming trend by saying the recent temperature rise is a natural and cyclical occurrence, but don't let them fool you. It's our industry and emissions that are changing the atmosphere, and only for the worse.

Notes

Summarizing

To review, summarizing allows you to employ another person's ideas and information to focus and strengthen your own writing. Professional writers and researchers make frequent use of their summarizing skills. On the TOEFL, you will use summaries to demonstrate your ability to take information from written and spoken passages and apply that information to a specific task. Here are several suggestions to guide you as you create a summary.

- A summary should always be briefer than the original essay or talk. A four- or five-paragraph essay, such as the "Global Warming" passage, should require no more than a paragraph to summarize. If your summary is more than about a quarter of the length of the original, look at your summary carefully to see if you can remove nonessential material.

- A summary should consist almost entirely of the main points of the original. There should be a minimum of examples and specific details.

- A summary should be written in your own words, rather than the words of the original writer or speaker. In other words, it should be *paraphrased*.

Paraphrasing

When you are using another person's ideas or information in your own essay, it is important to express them using your own words (paraphrasing), rather than simply writing things down exactly the way the writer did. There are several reasons for this. First, paraphrasing gives you an opportunity to practice and display your own English abilities. It allows you to make the work your own. Second, when you paraphrase, you are making certain that you really do understand what you've learned—by paraphrasing the material, you are helping yourself understand it better. Finally, paraphrasing allows you to avoid the ethical and legal issues created by plagiarism, which is using another author's exact words as if they were your own. Plagiarism is strictly discouraged in the academic and professional worlds, unless the borrowed phrasing is placed within quotation marks and its source is clearly identified.

There are several ways to approach paraphrasing. A good strategy is to find synonyms for the original terms. Refer again to the lecture transcript on global warming. For example, instead of using the word *predict* from the lecture, you could write *anticipate.* Instead of *accelerated warming,* you could write *faster heating.* Paraphrasing is a good way to expand your vocabulary.

Another strategy is to alter the sentence structure of the original. This works well in conjunction with your newly found synonyms. For example, the sentence, "While there have been large variations in temperature on Earth for thousands of years, the current warming trend is cause for alarm—and we only have ourselves to blame for it." could be reflected in your notes this way: "Earth has a history of large changes in temperature, but humans are responsible for the quickly rising temperatures we are experiencing today."

Practice paraphrasing from the "Global Warming" lecture in the space below.

_____

_____

_____

_____

_____

_____

_____

_____

_____

_____

_____

_____

_____

Following is a sample summary of the "Global Warming" lecture:

> The Earth has gone through large changes in temperature before, but they usually take a long time. Since the Industrial Revolution, the burning of fossil fuels and other materials has greatly increased the levels of CO_2 in our atmosphere, which naturally traps heat from the sun. The problem is that the rising levels of CO_2 trap more heat, which raises global temperatures quickly. Scientists predict that global warming will bring cause faster heating, with the earth's temperature going up as much as ten degrees over the next hundred years, in large part because of emissions from our industrial society.

Writing the Body of a Definition Essay

Now it's time to review some of the strategies and skills that will help you write an effective essay on test day.

Remember from Chapter 2 on writing that all the actual discussion in a definition essay takes place in its body paragraphs. In these paragraphs, you explain your ideas and provide all the information the reader needs to understand those ideas. Body paragraphs can contain a variety of different kinds of information, from statistics to dates to short narratives. In a definition essay, examples and explanations are most commonly found.

All body paragraphs should have certain features in common. These common features are a *topic sentence* and supporting details. With a little practice, you can learn to use these two parts of a paragraph to write strong, effective definition essays.

The Topic Sentence

Each body paragraph must have a topic sentence. Usually, this will be the first sentence of the paragraph and will specify the exact topic to be discussed. Ideally, each of these topics will have been mentioned in the introduction, in the same order in which they occur in the essay body. That will help the reader to navigate through the essay, by knowing exactly when and where you will be discussing each topic.

The better the reader can understand the structure of the essay, the easier the reader will understand the content of the essay. In a definition essay, perhaps even more than any other kind of essay, enabling the reader to understand is critically important. Topic sentences help you to achieve this goal.

Let's look at the following model essay about simple machines. First, read the introduction carefully, paying particular attention to the last sentence. This is the thesis statement of the essay. It refers to three different topics: levers, inclined planes, and pulleys.

Next, read the first sentence of each of the body paragraphs. These are the topic sentences. Each topic sentence introduces the topic to be discussed in that paragraph but provides only general information about it. Note that the three topics occur in the essay body in exactly the same order in which they are listed in the introductory paragraph.

Simple Machines

Have you ever used a bottle opener? Raised a flag to the top of a pole? Ridden a bicycle up a hill? If so, you have made use of an important category of human tools: simple machines. All simple machines have two common features: first, they must be structurally basic—it must be impossible to remove any component from the machine without destroying it—and second, they all work by changing the direction, magnitude, or travel of a moving force. This force is called the effort, or input, and the work the machine accomplishes is called its load. Though simple machines vary in size and form, all of them can be placed into one of three categories: levers, inclined planes, or pulleys.

The lever is the simple machine we see most often in our daily lives. A lever consists of a body of rigid material along which effort is transferred to the load. During its operation, one end of the lever may move, or its two ends may move in opposite directions. In either case, there will be a point somewhere along the length of the lever that is motionless. This point is called the fulcrum. Moving the fulcrum closer to the load increases the lever's mechanical advantage; moving the fulcrum closer to the effort decreases this advantage. Imagine using a bottle opener. The opener's tip is the fulcrum. The load—the edge of the bottle cap—is between the fulcrum and the effort (the user's hand). As the user pushes the opener upward, pulling the bottle cap with it, the lever transfers the effort to the bottle cap. If the user's hand rises by five centimeters, and the cap rises by one centimeter, then the magnitude of force applied at the load will be five times the original effort.

A good example of an inclined plane, the second most common simple machine, is a hilly road. If the road is very steep, climbing the hill on a bicycle is hard work; if the grade (or steepness) of the hill is reduced, the climb will be easier. If a hill ascends at a 45-degree angle, then a bicyclist who wants to gain 100 meters in altitude must travel 200 meters along the incline, twice the actual vertical distance, but the climb requires half the effort per meter. Thus, there is an inverse relationship between the effort required to raise a load using an inclined plane and the distance along the plane that must be traveled to raise the load the desired height.

Pulleys are more rare than either levers or inclined planes but are important simple machines nonetheless. A simple pulley consists of a grooved wheel and a rope passing over it and serves only to change the direction of force. For example, to lift a flag to the top of a flagpole, the rope is passed over the pulley at the top of the pole, and one end is attached to the flag. Then, when downward effort is applied to the other end of the rope, the flag is pulled upward. Each pulley can be mounted in a block with other pulleys, with the rope traveling back and forth between them. If one block is fixed and another is free and supporting the load, there results a mechanical advantage, or change in the magnitude of force. This change is a multiple of the total number of pulleys used. Thus, lifting a load of three tons with three pulleys requires the same initial effort as lifting one ton with one pulley; however, the point on the rope receiving the initial effort will need to travel three times as far.

The basic function of simple machines is to convert energy into work. At the heart of the function of these machines is motion, which is the source of input to the machine and is modified into the output. Levers, inclined planes, and pulleys can all be used to a mechanical advantage, but all exhibit a trade-off: the total amount of energy expended to do a task is always the same no matter how it is done, but the simple machine permits the energy expenditure to be distributed over a greater distance or time. This basic aspect of simple machines is why they are critical elements of everyday tasks. To unlatch a door or remove a bottle cap without the simple machine would be anything but simple.

Supporting Details

Because supporting details are so important, let's take some time to review them again.

After the topic sentence, each paragraph should include a number of supporting details. These details can take various forms: statistics, names and dates, short quotations, explanations, or examples. In a definition essay, the example is the most common kind of supporting information; explanatory sentences are also common.

Now, read each paragraph of the essay about simple machines from beginning to end. Notice that after each topic sentence, a number of supporting sentences provide more detailed information about the topic. Each paragraph contains at least one example and a number of additional sentences that explain how the example illustrates the topic of the paragraph.

Let's look more closely at body paragraph number two (the third paragraph in the essay). The topic sentence tells us the topic of the paragraph: inclined planes. It also suggests how the author intends to explain that topic: by showing how hilly roads are examples of inclined planes. The second sentence places the reader into a situation that most people have probably experienced, climbing a steep hill on a bicycle. We also know from experience that a steeper hill is harder to climb than a less steep one. Only after providing this familiar example does the writer attempt to explain the topic in terms of abstract mathematics or science, which many people find harder to understand than real-life examples. Thus, each sentence in this paragraph works to support the preceding ones.

Carefully chosen examples are always a strong addition to the discussion in any essay. A good example will be familiar to the reader or illustrate a process, principle, or idea with which the reader is already acquainted. Then, when the reader is trying to understand the writer's explanation, the example will permit the reader to relate the topic to his or her own experience, making the topic much more easily understood.

Now we can draw a model of a body paragraph. It should look something like this:

Topic sentence

↑

Supporting detail

↑

Supporting detail

↑

Supporting detail

Here's a rule to help you practice writing body paragraphs. A body paragraph should consist of at least four sentences, including the topic sentence. Having fewer sentences suggests that the paragraph is insufficiently developed and should contain more information. If you find that you have only two or three sentences about your paragraph topic and are not sure what else to say, consider whether this topic should be included in the essay at all or whether it would be more appropriate to connect it to another paragraph elsewhere in the essay. On the other hand, you may simply need to do more brainstorming on the underdeveloped topic.

The Conclusion

One part of the essay that often receives too little attention is the conclusion. In a timed writing situation, this is understandable, because you may have very little time to devote to writing a good conclusion. However, the conclusion is the second most important part of the essay, after the introduction. The conclusion is the last impression the reader has of you—and, of course, that should be a good impression. But conclusions don't have to be difficult or time consuming if you keep a couple of basic rules in mind.

- **Rule 1:** Conclusions do not need to be long. In fact, they shouldn't be. All of your information has already been presented in the body of the essay. Don't introduce new information in the conclusion.

- **Rule 2:** The conclusion has a very clear task, which is to remind the reader what was important about the discussion and what lesson or message should be taken from the essay. This should be done in a fresh way. Simply summarizing the discussion or repeating the thesis can be helpful, but neither makes a good conclusion all by itself.

Let's look at the model essay about simple machines one more time.

Simple Machines

Have you ever used a bottle opener? Raised a flag to the top of a pole? Ridden a bicycle up a hill? If so, you have made use of an important category of human tools: simple machines. All simple machines have two common features: first, they must be structurally basic—it must be impossible to remove any component from the machine without destroying it—and second, they all work by changing the direction, magnitude, or travel of a moving force. This force is called the effort, or input, and the work the machine accomplishes is called its load. Though simple machines vary in size and form, all of them can be placed into one of three categories: levers, inclined planes, or pulleys.

The lever is the simple machine we see most often in our daily lives. A lever consists of a body of rigid material along which effort is transferred to the load. During its operation, one end of the lever may move, or its two ends may move in opposite directions. In either case, there will be a point somewhere along the length of the lever that is motionless. This point is called the fulcrum. Moving the fulcrum closer to the load increases the lever's mechanical advantage; moving the fulcrum closer to the effort decreases this advantage. Imagine using a bottle opener. The opener's tip is the fulcrum. The load—the edge of the bottle cap—is between the fulcrum and the effort (the user's hand). As the user pushes the opener upward, pulling the bottle cap with it, the lever transfers the effort to the bottle cap. If the user's hand rises by five centimeters, and the cap rises by one centimeter, then the magnitude of force applied at the load will be five times the original effort.

A good example of an inclined plane, the second most common simple machine, is a hilly road. If the road is very steep, climbing the hill on a bicycle is hard work; if the grade (or steepness) of the hill is reduced, the climb will be easier. If a hill ascends at a 45-degree angle, then a bicyclist who wants to gain 100 meters in altitude must travel 200 meters along the incline, twice the actual vertical distance, but the climb requires half the effort per meter. Thus, there is an inverse relationship between the effort required to raise a load using an inclined plane and the distance along the plane that must be traveled to raise the load the desired height.

Pulleys are more rare than either levers or inclined planes but are important simple machines nonetheless. A simple pulley consists of a grooved wheel and a rope passing over it and serves only to change the direction of force. For example, to lift a flag to the top of a flagpole, the rope is passed over the pulley at the top of the pole, and one end is attached to the flag. Then, when downward effort is applied to the other end of the rope, the flag is pulled upward. Each pulley can be mounted in a block with other pulleys, with the rope traveling back and forth between them. If one block is fixed and another is free and supporting the load, there results a mechanical advantage or change in the magnitude of force. This change is a multiple of the total number of pulleys used. Thus, lifting a load of three tons with three pulleys requires the same initial effort as lifting one ton with one pulley; however, the point on the rope receiving the initial effort will need to travel three times as far.

The basic function of simple machines is to convert energy into work. At the heart of the function of these machines is motion, which is the source of input to the machine and is modified into the output. Levers, inclined planes, and pulleys can all be used to a mechanical advantage, but all exhibit a trade-off: the total amount of energy expended to do a task is always the same no matter how it is done, but the simple machine permits the energy expenditure to be distributed over a greater distance or time. This basic aspect of simple machines is why they are critical elements of everyday tasks. To unlatch a door or remove a bottle cap without the simple machine would be anything but simple.

The conclusion of the essay is one of the two shortest paragraphs in the essay. No new information is included in this paragraph. Instead, the conclusion reviews the characteristics common to all simple machines and summarizes the principles that underlie their operation. Finally, the conclusion closes by reminding the reader why simple machines are an important part of our everyday lives.

In the following Essay Practice, try to remember these two rules, and you may find the task of writing the concluding paragraph of your essay to be much easier than you expected.

PRACTICE: ESSAY WRITING

Now you will read a passage, listen to part of a lecture, and write a response. This activity is similar to the first of two writing tasks that will be on the TOEFL.

> You will have three minutes to read the following passage. You may take notes.

Outsourcing

Many American companies have decided to outsource jobs performed by Americans to workers in other countries. This issue has fast become controversial, as some advocates of outsourcing see it as the only way to keep their companies competitive. Opponents of outsourcing view it as the number-one reason for unemployment in the United States. Who's right?

Multinational companies first began to outsource as a way to gain visibility in foreign markets where American workers were unfamiliar with the local business customs. As time passed, the combination of skilled workers and low wages led American companies to support the infrastructure in these countries with an eye to moving nonessential operations to these locations eventually.

In reality, this shift of such operations as telemarketing and customer service closely parallels a shift that occurred 25 to 30 years ago, when U.S. companies moved these same operations from cities to rural areas within the United States where labor was less expensive. That sort of domestic outsourcing also raised eyebrows at the time, but many people today feel that it's completely acceptable for a company's headquarters to be located in New York City while its lower-wage positions are in smaller cities where the cost of labor and operating budgets is much lower. This is simply good business sense—keeping costs low and production high—and makes products and services more affordable.

Those who view outsourcing as responsible for the loss of U.S. jobs are terribly misguided. Outsourcing is a valid business proposition that has the best interests of the U.S. public in mind. By sending operations offshore, American companies are securing their own financial future and that of the American public—not causing rampant unemployment.

Notes

Now that you've read the passage, ask a friend or a fellow student to read the following transcript to you.

🔊 **Writing, Essay Practice—Lecture Transcript**

Narrator: Now listen to part of a talk on the topic you just read about.

Professor: As more and more companies have gone "global," there's been a huge increase in the number of employees based outside of the United States. The trend is for companies to decentralize operations, making the move from manufacturing an entire TV, say, to focusing only on the company's core competencies . . . Maybe it manufactures just the TV screen rather than the complete TV, as it did 20 years ago.

This increased specialization results in companies taking their noncore operations and shipping them to some other country, where skilled labor costs a fraction of what it does here in the United States.

So what does this mean for the American working public? By taking various operations—including sales and customer service—away from the United States, companies are flat out removing jobs from our economy. As larger companies shift their information technology services, call centers, and other operations to cheaper jurisdictions, everyone performing those functions here in the United States loses their jobs. Generally, working-class people lose their jobs, while upper management remains untouched. In some cases, yes, outsourcing makes a company more profitable, which should benefit employees in the long run but, more often than not, just results in lost jobs.

Outsourcing is a fact of life, and we can't escape it. The only way we can help protect American jobs is by encouraging companies to educate the workers whose jobs are moving offshore.

If companies commit to building the skill sets and experience of workers here in the United States, there's a chance that they'll also award these employees with better-paying positions once their current jobs are outsourced. If that happens, outsourcing will be a win-win situation for everyone involved.

Notes

You have 20 minutes to plan and write your response. Your response will be judged on the basis of the quality of your writing and on how well your response presents the points in the lecture and their relationship to the reading passage. Typically, an effective response will be 150–225 words.

⬤ **Writing, Essay Prompt**

> Summarize the points made in the lecture you just heard, and then compare the speaker's opinion with the opinion stated in the reading.

_____

_____

_____

_____

_____

_____

_____

_____

_____

_____

_____

_____

_____

_____

_____

_____

_____

_____

Answer: You may compare your essay to the sample essay here. Note that there can be many acceptable variations for this essay response.

Sample Essay: Outsourcing

Many companies in the United States are changing the way that they do business. Instead of focusing on the creation of a whole product, they are building their businesses around manufacturing parts of products, then supplying other companies. This is intended to maximize profit, but it also has a negative effect on employment in the United States.

This business strategy has led companies to move their manufacturing operations to parts of the world where costs are much lower than in the United States. Outsourcing of things like call centers and technology services has led to lost U.S. jobs, especially in nonmanagement positions. Because of the money being saved, outsourcing is unavoidable. But if U.S. companies give their employees new skills before sending their jobs overseas, then outsourcing will not necessarily have such a negative impact.

Another view of outsourcing is that it is an established business strategy that has already been used successfully. Companies in the United States used a similar strategy about 25 years ago, when many of them moved their manufacturing plants from cities to less expensive rural areas. The companies were able to save money and create new jobs for people who needed them. This meant the companies were able to positively contribute to the economy. The only difference is that when companies outsource nowadays, they are doing it on a global, not national, scale.

When you're ready, move on to the next chapter.

Chapter 7:
Listening: Implication and Inference, Context and Tone

Implication and Inference

These two terms are essential to your understanding of some of the listening questions on the TOEFL.

An *implication* is the meaning of a statement that is not obvious in the literal meaning of the words. If you have been studying for a test with a fellow student for many hours and you want to stop, you might say, "I'm tired." Literally, you are stating that you are feeling a lack of energy, but you are *implying* that you want to stop studying.

An *inference* is the act of drawing a conclusion based on evidence. If you say, "I'm tired," and you mean that you want to stop studying, your fellow student must *infer* your meaning. Sometimes one must consider more than just one statement from a speaker to draw an inference.

Context and Tone

Context refers to information presented before and after a statement or the setting in which a statement is uttered. Context is important in determining the meaning of a speaker's implication and in drawing inferences based on several pieces of information. In saying, "I'm tired," to a fellow student with whom you've been studying, the context is the fact that you have been studying for several hours. This fact helps your fellow student infer that you may want to stop studying.

Tone refers to the way in which a statement is uttered. Tone is also important in determining the meaning of a speaker's implication. If you say, "I'm tired," with a tone of finality, this tone helps your fellow student understand that you want to stop studying.

Rhetorical and Interrogative Questions

Context and tone are also important in understanding the two general types of questions: **rhetorical** and **interrogative**. An interrogative question is asked to gather information. When someone asks an interrogative question, that person wants an answer. *Rhetoric* is the art of speaking or writing to persuade. A rhetorical question is one designed to influence the listener. No answer is expected when a rhetorical question is asked.

Context and tone are usually required to distinguish the difference between an interrogative and rhetorical question. For example, the question, "How old are you?" can be either rhetorical or interrogative given the circumstances. Two children getting to know each other often want to find out each other's age. Under these circumstances, the child asking, "How old are you?" is asking an interrogative question. Most likely, the child would stress the word *old* when asking the question. Now, let's say that a college student is misbehaving in class. Because of that student's childish behavior, the professor might ask the same question but with an emphasis on the word *how* or *are*. This gives the question a tone of sarcasm. The professor doesn't really want to know the student's age. The professor is trying to discourage the student's bad behavior by implying that the student is acting like a child.

Other purposes of rhetorical questions are:

- **To express an opinion.** "Isn't he foolish?" in response to a pedestrian carelessly crossing the street in front of your car.
- **To express a feeling.** "How could I forget again?" shows frustration in response to the second time you forgot to call your mother on her birthday.
- **To give a command.** "Shall we get back to work now?" might be a manager's instruction to employees after a long lunch.

PRACTICE: LISTENING QUESTIONS

There are several different question types on the Listening section of the TOEFL. Chapter 3 covered the following types:

- Understanding rhetorical function
- Drawing an inference

This chapter will review drawing an inference questions and will also cover another question type:

- Understanding a speaker's implication

Question Type 3 Review—Drawing an Inference

There are two or three conversations and four to six lectures in the Listening section of the TOEFL. Again, inference questions ask you to draw conclusions about specific details in the passage or to make comparisons between details. To answer these types of inference questions, you should:

- Listen carefully to the details of the lecture or conversation
- Try to understand unfamiliar words from context
- Listen for conditionals, intonation, and suggestions made by the speakers while the conversation is happening so that you can anticipate certain inference questions
- Use your knowledge about the situation to guess what sort of conclusion might be logical

The following are examples of inference questions:

- What probably happened to _____ ?
- What will _____ probably do next?
- What can be inferred about _____ ?

Now answer the following questions. Remember that on the actual test, you will only hear the excerpt—you will not be able to read it. If you want to get the most out of this listening practice, do **NOT** simply read the excerpt. You might have a native speaker read the excerpt aloud to you, or have the native speaker record a reading of the excerpt that you can play. Remember, also, that the question and the four answer choices in listening questions appear on the computer screen, but only the question is spoken by the narrator.

> **Narrator:** Listen again to part of the discussion. Then answer the question.
>
> **Professor:** Sweets are no more out of bounds to people with diabetes than they are to the rest of us, especially if they are eaten as part of a healthy diet and exercise plan.
>
> What can be inferred from the speaker's statement?
>
> (A) Sweets should not be eaten by people with diabetes.
>
> (B) Diabetics need to eat a certain amount of sweet foods.
>
> (C) Diabetics need to plan out their meals weeks ahead of time to lose weight.
>
> (D) People with diabetes can eat sweets if they are careful.

Answer: Choice (A) is a distracter that appeals to the definition of *out-of-bounds* as *not allowed*. Choice (B) is incorrect because the speaker is not discussing a specific diet for diabetics. Choice (C) is playing with the word *plan* as a verb instead of a noun. Choice (D) is correct because the phrase *no more out of bounds* implies that sweet foods are acceptable for diabetics, if consumed in a healthy way.

> **Narrator:** Listen again to part of the discussion. Then answer the question.
>
> **Pat:** . . . when the body cannot convert blood glucose into energy, what does it do? Any ideas . . . ? Okay, it begins to break down stored fat to use for fuel. And this can cause problems, because using too much fat for fuel can lead to high blood pressure and strokes.
>
> Based on the speaker's comments, what can be inferred about glucose?
>
> Ⓐ It can break down fat for energy.
>
> Ⓑ It can be measured by analyzing brain function.
>
> Ⓒ It can affect how the body fuels itself.
>
> Ⓓ It can aid in storing fat.

Answer: Choice (A) is incorrect because glucose provides energy to the body but does not break down fat. (B) is incorrect because there is no mention of measuring glucose by analyzing brain function. Choice (D) is incorrect because no evidence supports this statement. Choice (C) is correct because the speaker explicitly mentions that low glucose levels can make the body begin to break down stored fat.

The next two questions require you to draw an inference based on your understanding of an entire lecture.

Refer to the following transcript, "Biology Class: Diabetes." Have a friend read the lecture aloud to you. Then, answer the questions that follow.

🔊 Listening Practice—Lecture Transcript

Narrator: Listen to part of a talk in a biology class.

Professor: All right, today's topic is diabetes. Diabetes is a disease marked by high levels of glucose in the blood. Now, can someone tell me what blood glucose is?

Student A: It's blood sugar, right?

Professor: Yes, the cells of our bodies use blood glucose, blood sugar, as a source of energy. However, before our bodies can use this blood glucose, it must move from the bloodstream into our individual cells. And this process requires a protein called insulin, which is produced by the pancreas. Insulin helps blood glucose move from the bloodstream into individual cells, so your body can use it for energy. Questions . . . ? [Pause] Okay, so what is diabetes? Diabetes occurs when the body doesn't produce enough insulin or when the body is unable to use insulin properly. With low insulin levels, it becomes very difficult for your body to use blood glucose for energy. And when the body cannot convert blood glucose into energy, what does it do? Any ideas . . . ? Okay, it begins to break down stored fat to use for fuel. And this can cause problems, because using too much fat for fuel can lead to high blood pressure and strokes. So high blood sugar really is a killer—

Student B: Excuse me, um . . . how exactly does high blood sugar damage you?

Professor: Lots of ways. First, your kidneys. Your kidneys remove impurities from the blood—that's their job. When you have extra glucose in the blood, this glucose passes through the kidneys, but the kidneys can't get rid of it all. Because not all of the extra glucose is removed by the kidneys, this excess glucose—accompanied by water—spills into the urine. The body tries to get rid of this glucose and water mix and this causes frequent urination, excessive thirst, and hunger. If diabetes isn't treated, it can cause further complications, including kidney failure . . . and there are other things, like blindness and heart disease. Now presently, there is no cure for diabetes, but—yes, Margaret?

Student A: But they say that foods with high sugar contents can cause diabetes. So, so wouldn't cutting down on sweets help get rid of diabetes?

Professor: It's surprising how many people "know" that diet is solely responsible for the development of diabetes. Actually, diabetes is caused by a combination of genetic and environmental factors. Sweets are no more out of bounds to people with diabetes than they are to the rest of us, especially if they are eaten as part of a healthy diet and exercise plan. On top of that, people who take insulin to treat their diabetes may sometimes need to eat high-sugar foods to prevent their blood glucose levels from falling too low. Now as I was saying, there is no cure for diabetes. So a person with diabetes must control the amount of glucose in their blood through regular physical exercise, a carefully controlled diet, and medication. They may require insulin injections a few times a day to provide the body with the insulin it doesn't produce.

And this can be tricky! You see, our bodies don't require a constant amount of insulin; the amount we need actually varies. So diabetics typically have to measure the level of glucose in a drop of their blood several times each day. If the blood glucose level is too high or too low, they can adjust the amount of insulin injected, as well as the amount of physical exercise they do or their food intake, to maintain a normal blood glucose level.

Student B: What happens if a person with diabetes injects too much insulin?

Professor: If a person with diabetes injects too much insulin, it can produce low blood sugar levels. This can lead to hypoglycemia, a condition characterized by shakiness, confusion, and anxiety. Anyone here ever felt like that after a long day? Maybe you needed a little snack.

Student B: So low insulin levels mean blood sugar levels get too high, but overly high insulin levels means your blood sugar level drops too low.

Professor: That's right. You want insulin levels that are neither too high nor too low.

Student A: So let's say a diabetic injects too much insulin, and now they drop to where their blood sugar is too low. What should they do?

Student B: You said it earlier: they should eat sweets . . . try to boost their blood sugar levels, right?

Professor: Yes, by consuming foods with sugar, such as fruit juice or sugar candy, many diabetics can eliminate hypoglycemic symptoms.

Great! That about covers how diabetes affects the body. Even today, scientists are unsure of the exact cause of diabetes. It continues to be a mystery, although both genetics and environmental factors such as obesity and lack of exercise appear to play roles. Fortunately, it seems that no matter what the cause is, many diabetics are able to manage their symptoms by following the same essential steps.

Notes

What will the professor probably do next?

(A) Introduce another symptom of diabetes

(B) Describe how many diabetics are able to manage their symptoms

(C) Debate the pros and cons of different methods of treating diabetes

(D) Explain which foods can cause diabetes

Answer: Answering this question successfully requires an understanding of the entire lecture. At one point in the lecture, the professor says, "Great! That about covers how diabetes affects the body," which implies that diabetes has been fully described. So, choice (A) would not be a good inference. Choice (C) would mean that several competing treatment options had been fully described, and that the professor had already described the pros and cons of each method. Choice (D) is an example of a statement that the doctor corrected during his talk. He states that diabetes is caused by a combination of "genetic and environmental factors." It's logical to assume that the reason they're talking about diabetes is for the professor to inform the students; therefore, choice (B) is the correct inference because, logically, the next part of the lecture should be about how people with diabetes manage their symptoms.

With which of the following statements would the professor probably agree?

Ⓐ Diabetes is caused by eating certain types of food.

Ⓑ People with diabetes can regulate their blood sugar by exercise alone.

Ⓒ Medicine is the only sure way to control insulin levels.

Ⓓ It is possible to control blood sugar levels by adopting a healthy lifestyle.

Answer: This question tests your ability to make an inference based on several pieces of information within the entire lecture. Choice (A) is incorrect because, toward the end of the lecture, the professor states that the exact cause of diabetes is not clear. Choices (B) and (C) both make incorrect assumptions about what the professor said. He stated several times that a combination of exercise, diet, and medicine were necessary to control insulin. Choice (D) is the correct answer. The professor implies this in his closing statement, "Fortunately, it seems that no matter what the cause is, many diabetics are able to manage their symptoms by following the same essential steps."

Question Type 3: Understanding a Speaker's Implication

There are two or three conversations and four to six lectures in the Listening section of the TOEFL. The answer choices for *speaker's implication* questions will contain situations that will further challenge you because they were not discussed or did not occur. You will also see synonyms (two words with a similar meaning), homophones (two words that sound the same but have different meanings), or other words repeated in the answer choices that are either out of context or not stated in the conversation.

The following are examples of implication questions:

- What does the man probably mean?
- What does the man suggest/imply?
- What does the woman want to know?
- Why does _____ say _____ ?
- What does _____ mean by _____ ?

Narrator: Listen again to part of the discussion. Then answer the question.

Professor: It's surprising how many people "know" that diet is solely responsible for the development of diabetes. Actually, diabetes is caused by a combination of genetic and environmental factors.

What does the speaker imply about many people?

(A) Some people should know that sweets are unhealthy.

(B) Some people believe that sweets with organically grown sugar do not cause diabetes.

(C) Some people incorrectly think that sugary foods are the cause of diabetes.

(D) Some people already know that eating sweets can cause diabetes.

Answer: Choice (A) is not an implication that the speaker made. The professor did not say that sweets were "healthy" or "unhealthy." In choice (B), we don't know from the context whether natural sugars are any better than other sugars. Choice (C) is correct, with the key being the emphasis placed on the word *know*, followed by *Actually* in the next sentence. The professor is pointing out that many people make an incorrect assumption about the connection between diet and diabetes. Choice (D) tries to distract with the literal idea of having knowledge about something, communicated by the word know which you might have chosen had you not identified the sarcasm.

Narrator: Listen again to part of the discussion. Then answer the question.

Professor: They may require insulin injections a few times a day to provide the body with the insulin it doesn't produce.

And this can be tricky! You see, our bodies don't require a constant amount of insulin; the amount we need actually varies.

What does the speaker mean when saying the following:

Professor: "And this can be tricky!"

(A) Controlling blood sugar levels is like performing magic.

(B) Maintaining healthy insulin levels throughout the day is not easy.

(C) Diabetics cannot give themselves insulin without a doctor's assistance.

(D) Determining the correct amount of insulin for an injection is not difficult.

Answer: Choice (A) is testing whether you understand the meaning of the word *tricky.* Choice (C) would be taking an inference too far. You would have to get more information before you arrived at this conclusion. Choice (D) is the opposite of what he's implying. Choice (B) is the correct answer. The speaker is stating that maintaining proper blood glucose levels requires knowledge and timing.

Narrator: Listen again to part of the discussion. Then answer the question.

Professor: Anyone here ever felt like that after a long day? Maybe you needed a little snack.

Why does the professor say this?

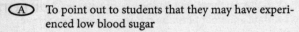 (A) To point out to students that they may have experienced low blood sugar

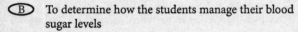 (B) To determine how the students manage their blood sugar levels

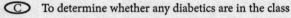 (C) To determine whether any diabetics are in the class

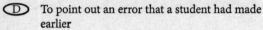 (D) To point out an error that a student had made earlier

Answer: In choice (D), if the student had made a mistake, the speaker would indicate this with different wording. Choices (B) and (C) are both distracters that look attractive as answers to a standard interrogative. However, this is a rhetorical question, and the speaker's tone is demonstrative. Choice (A) is the correct answer, because the tone of the speaker's rhetorical question communicates that the professor is providing information to the students.

When you're ready, move on to the next chapter, "Speaking: Expressing and Supporting an Opinion."

Chapter 8:
Speaking: Expressing and Supporting an Opinion

Remember that in the last chapter about speaking, we covered two tasks:

1. Describing something from your own experience

2. Summarizing a lecture

This chapter covers two more speaking tasks:

1. Expressing and supporting an opinion based on personal experience

2. Summarizing a conversation and expressing an opinion

Before we review these tasks, let's review an important skill you should already be familiar with: paraphrasing.

Paraphrasing

In the TOEFL, you will listen to presentations. You will then be asked to summarize the information in the presentation (that is, give a short version that includes the main ideas and some supporting ideas but no specific details, examples, etc.) Earlier, in Chapter 6 on writing, you learned that summarizing often requires the skill of paraphrasing—that is, expressing someone else's ideas using your own words. To paraphrase, it is helpful to know synonyms. Synonyms are words that are similar in meaning.

Understanding the speaking tasks is critical for knowing how and where you can apply your strategies. Keep reading to learn more.

PRACTICE: SPEAKING TASKS

There are six tasks in the Speaking section of the TOEFL. The second type requires you to speak for 45 seconds while giving and supporting an opinion based on your personal experience.

You will both listen to and hear a speaking prompt. You will then have 15 seconds to prepare a spoken response of 45 seconds. Remember that you will not see the narrator's introduction to the question on the test.

Here is a list of phrases that can be used to state an opinion.

- I believe . . .
- I agree with the idea of . . . ing
- I don't think . . .
- I think . . .
- I agree that it is important to . . .
- I disagree with the idea of . . .
- I feel . . .
- I support the idea of . . . ing
- If you ask me . . .
- Some people might say . ., but I think . . .

Practice the following sample TOEFL question. Remember that you will not see the narrator's introduction to the question on the test. If you have a study partner or someone who can listen to your response, ask that person to read the transcript for "The Future of Printed Books." When you respond to the sample question, be sure to state and support your opinion.

The Future of Printed Books

Narrator: In this question, you will be asked to state and support your opinion about an issue. After you hear the question, you will have 15 seconds to prepare your response and 45 seconds to speak.

Some people think that television, the Internet, and other electronic media make the printed book obsolete as a source of information or entertainment. Other people say that printed books will continue to play an important role in society. Which view do you agree with? Include details and examples in your explanation.

15 seconds to prepare   45 seconds to speak.

Notes

Evaluate yourself using the following criteria:

Criteria	Comments	Action to Improve
Clarity and pronunciation		
Organization		
Details and examples		
Grammar and vocabulary		

Now ask your study partner to read the sample response aloud. How is it different from yours? How is it similar?

Sample Response: The Future of Printed Books

Okay, so electronic media. Will it make printed words obsolete? Well, in my opinion it will. I think that media like television and the Internet are quickly becoming more important for a couple of different reasons. For one thing, TV and the Internet are both really easy to access for almost anyone. As long as you . . . um . . . as long as you can get a TV signal or if you can connect to the Internet. Television is better because you can get local and international news and watch programs that are entertaining to you. With a book, you can choose a particular topic that you like, but usually books are only about one subject. You can't change channels and watch something else if you get bored. The Internet is especially a threat to books and newspapers because you can ask it questions and look for information on your own. In a magazine or newspaper, you might find lots of different interesting ideas, but if you want to know more about them, you have to go somewhere else. The only drawback that TVs and the Internet have is that, right now, they are not quite as portable and easy to use as newspapers and books. But I think that TV and the Internet will become more convenient in the near future.

Task 5: Summarizing a Conversation and Expressing an Opinion

There are six tasks in the Speaking section of the TOEFL. The fifth requires that you summarize a conversation in which two people are discussing a problem, then give your opinion on a solution.

In the fifth task in the Speaking section, you will listen to a conversation between two people. The two people generally discuss a topic related to life at a university. The topic is framed as a problem, and at least two solutions or attitudes to the problem are presented during the conversation.

As you listen to the conversation, remember that you will have to do the following in your response:

- Identify the topic the speakers are discussing
- Summarize the two (or more) solutions or opinions that the speakers express, making sure to paraphrase what the speakers say
- Present your own opinion on the topic
- Justify your opinion or say why you have that opinion

Now practice the following TOEFL question. Remember that you will not see the narrator's introduction to the question on the test. If you have a study partner or someone who can listen to your response, ask that person to read the transcript for "Switching Advisors."

Switching Advisors

Narrator: In this question, you will listen to a conversation. You will then answer a question about it. After you hear the question, you will have 20 seconds to prepare your response and 60 seconds to speak.

Narrator: Now listen to a conversation between two students.

Student A: Nadine, you gotta minute? I could use some advice.

Student B: What's the trouble, Sean?

Student A: I'm thinking of switching advisors . . .

Student B: I don't get it. You were so excited when Dr. Henderson was assigned to be your advisor. Isn't he some kind of big shot?

Student A: Yeah, he won a big chem prize a couple of years ago, and they say he has a good chance to win a Nobel Prize in the next couple of years.

Student B: So, your advisor's a genius. You should be happy.

Student A: I am, I guess. It's just that . . . well . . . I never get to see him. He's never around. He's always off attending some international conference. His *assistant* gave the last two lectures.

Student B: Ah, the "Case of the Missing Professor."

Student A: So I'm thinking of switching to another advisor, one I can have more contact with. But I can't decide.

Student B: A recommendation letter from Henderson would sure help you get into grad school. But he's not gonna recommend you if he doesn't get to know you first. Why don't you write to him? Tell him you're really interested in his research. Ask if you could help out in his lab in some way. I'm sure he'd welcome an eager helper.

Student A: You think? I'm just a sophomore. I'm thinking I should find another professor in the department who'd take me under his wing and maybe even help me, you know, make contacts in the field. In the end, that might be a lot more useful.

Student B: I think you're selling yourself short. Show some initiative and make yourself known to him. High-profile people like him respect go-getters. Even if you don't learn anything from him directly, his endorsement could open a lot of doors for you.

Student A: Yeah, but I'd sure like to get some feedback and learn something from my advisor, too. It shouldn't all be politics.

Notes

> The students discuss two possible solutions to the man's
> problem. Describe the problem. Then state which solution
> you prefer and explain why.
>
> | 20 seconds to prepare | 60 seconds to speak. |

Evaluate yourself using the following criteria:

- Clarity and pronunciation
- Organization
- Details and examples
- Grammar and vocabulary

Now ask your study partner to read the sample response aloud. How
is it different from yours? How is it similar?

Sample Response: Switching Advisors

One of the students explains that his university advisor is not meeting his expectations. The advisor is famous
and has a great reputation, but he is not available to his
students. In fact, the student says that the professor's
assistant has been teaching his classes for him. That is ter-
rible, and it would make me mad as well. He is thinking
of getting another advisor. The other student suggests that
he should write a letter to his advisor and see if he can
get some kind of job working for him. She says that the
student should try to show the professor that he is smart
and a hard worker to get a recommendation for graduate
school. I think that this is an excellent idea. Another professor might be able to offer more direct help, but if he is
able to work for this professor, he might have a chance to
get to know the professor personally. A recommendation
from a successful professor will be a very strong part of
the student's application to graduate school, and he might
work on some projects that are very important and good
for his career.

Great job! You have finished your second reading, writing, listening, and speaking chapters. When you are ready, turn to Part 4 to learn more skills and strategies for mastering the TOEFL.

Part Four
Integrated Skills

Part Four delves into more complex topics of English language usage, including details, nuances of conversation, and techniques for persuasive writing. Make sure to complete all the practice exercises and sample questions so that you can get the most out of this part

Chapter 9:
Reading: Details

Transitions and Coherence

A transition from one paragraph to the next involves changing the reader's focus from one idea to another. In addition to using transitional expressions (*next, then, in addition, in conclusion,* etc.), you can make a transition flow more smoothly for the reader by using other techniques. Here are some of those techniques:

- Repetition of a word
- Use of a synonym of a word
- Use of pronouns
- Use of determiners (*the, this, that, these, those, their,* etc.)
- Definition, development, or contrast of a key word

These techniques are used both within a paragraph and between paragraphs to make the text flow more smoothly.

Look at some examples within a paragraph from the text that follows:

The **learning** theories that dominated the first half of the 20th century came predominantly from the *behavioral school of psychology.* Behaviorists view learning as a function of environmental factors that promote associations between stimuli and responses. Drawing on the animal experiments of Pavlov, who showed how dogs could *learn* to associate the sound of a bell with food, early behaviorists saw learning as a product of conditioning—that is—the repeated performance of an act, usually in the interest of some external reward. This led the behaviorists to conclude that *learning* is essentially *the* repetition of externally reinforced behaviors.

What do you notice about the use of repetition, synonyms, pronouns, determiners, and the definition, development, or contrast of key words?

Cohesive Devices

There are many different ways to transition smoothly between sentences when writing. These transitional words and phrases are called *cohesive devices.* The following passages include commonly used cohesive devices. They are highlighted in **italics.**

Pronouns

While psychologists tend to agree that learning plays a vital role in human functioning, **they** have developed very different perspectives, or theories, on its causes, processes, and consequences.

Demonstrative Pronouns

Drawing on the animal experiments of Pavlov, who showed how dogs could learn to associate the sound of a bell with food, early behaviorists saw learning as a product of conditioning—that is, the repeated performance of an act, usually in the interest of some external reward. **This** led the behaviorists to conclude that learning is essentially the repetition of externally reinforced behaviors.

Demonstrative Adjectives

Once the behavior of a model is observed, the input received must be cognitively processed and retained in the form of a general rule. **This general rule** undergoes constant revision based on future observations of others as well as the input received from others regarding the performer's behavior.

Articles

The early research findings of Bandura and his colleagues challenged **the** prevailing view of learning by demonstrating that it is not necessary to perform **a** behavior to learn **the** behavior and that reinforcement is not **a** necessary component of learning.

Transitional Phrases

Features of the task being modeled are another variable that influences attention. **Thus** teachers will often use bright colors, music, or odd shapes to encourage children to attend to their lessons.

Repetition, Synonym, or Slight Variation of a Word

The four subprocesses involved in **observational learning** are attention, retention, production, and motivation. For **observational learning** to occur, a person must be exposed to the behaviors of models within their daily lives and be capable of and willing to pay attention to these behaviors.

OR

Alfred Bandura began his research on observational learning in the early 1960s as a reaction to the behaviorist **viewpoint** on learning. The early research findings of Bandura and his colleagues challenged the prevailing **view** of learning by demonstrating that it is not necessary to perform a behavior to learn the behavior and that reinforcement is not a necessary component of learning.

OR

Modeling is a major construct of the theory and refers to the fact that people learn by observing the behavior of others and the response that the behaviors elicit from those around them. When people observe the consequences of **modeled behaviors**, they gain information regarding the appropriateness of these behaviors.

PRACTICE: READING QUESTIONS:

Understanding the question types is important for knowing how and where you can apply your strategies. There are several question types on the Reading section of the TOEFL. We have already reviewed five types in Chapters 1 and 5. These are:

1. Drawing an inference

2. Summarizing the most important points

3. Understanding rhetorical function

4. Understanding details

5. Understanding details as they relate to the main idea (schematic table)

In this chapter, we will review three more types:

1. Inferring word meaning from context

2. Locating a referent

3. Understanding coherence

It is critical to understand what each of these question types are testing as well as how they are presented.

Question Type 6: Inferring Word Meaning from Context

There are three to five passages in the Reading section of the TOEFL. Each passage is followed by three to five word meaning questions.

Having an extensive vocabulary is extremely important in understanding the meaning of a text or lecture, but sometimes the meaning of new words can be inferred from the context. Some typical techniques for inferring the meaning of words are:

- Looking for examples
- Looking for contrasting words or ideas
- Identifying synonyms or an explanation in other parts of the passage

Read the following passage and then look at the three examples taken from it. For now, ignore the symbols that appear in the text; these apply to questions you will answer later in this section under question type 10.

The Social Cognitive Theory of Learning

Learning is an important aspect of virtually all areas of life. From infancy through old age, people must learn to talk, read, play, work, and **get along** socially in society. Due to its pervasive nature, learning has long been a topic of intense study within psychology. While psychologists tend to agree that learning plays a vital role in human functioning, they have developed very different perspectives, or **theories,** on its causes, processes, and consequences.

The learning theories that dominated the first half of the 20th century came predominantly from the behavioral school of psychology. Behaviorists view learning as a function of environmental factors that promote associations between stimuli and responses. Drawing on the animal experiments of Pavlov, who showed how dogs could learn to associate the sound of a bell with food, early behaviorists saw learning as a product of conditioning—that is, the repeated performance of an act, usually in the interest of some external reward. This led the behaviorists to conclude that learning is essentially the repetition of externally reinforced behaviors.

Alfred Bandura began his research on observational learning in the early 1960s as a reaction to the behaviorist viewpoint on learning. The early research findings of Bandura and his colleagues challenged the prevailing view of learning by demonstrating that it is not necessary to perform a behavior to learn the behavior and that reinforcement is not a necessary component of learning. Social cognitive theory was developed by Bandura to provide a comprehensive explanation of observational learning.

[▲] (A) Bandura's social cognitive theory is based on the assumption that the majority of human learning occurs within a social environment. [▲] (B) **Modeling** is a major construct of the theory and refers to the fact that people learn by observing the behavior of others and the response that the behaviors elicit from those around them. [▲] (C) When people observe the consequences of modeled behaviors, they gain information regarding the appropriateness of these behaviors. [▲] (D) Research on modeling has been used to explain how people learn a variety of skills, beliefs, strategies, and knowledge.

The three functions of modeling proposed by Bandura's social cognitive theory are response facilitation, inhibition/disinhibition, and observational learning. Response facilitation involves the modeling of socially acceptable behavior. The modeled behavior tends to include social prompts that motivate the observer to perform the modeled behavior. Inhibition/disinhibition involves the modeling of socially unacceptable behavior. During inhibition, the model receives punishment as a consequence for performing a prohibited behavior, and the observer is discouraged from performing the behavior. On the other hand, during disinhibition, the prohibited behavior being modeled does not result in a negative consequence for the model, and the observer is encouraged to perform the unacceptable behavior. Observational learning occurs when an observer performs a new behavior that they would not have performed prior to observing the behavior modeled.

The four subprocesses involved in observational learning are attention, retention, production, and motivation. For observational learning to occur, a person must be exposed to the behaviors of models within their daily lives and be capable of and willing to pay attention to these behaviors. [■] (A) The specific characteristics of the model will influence how effective a model is at attracting attention. [■] (B) People generally attend to models and modes of behavior that they regard as similar to themselves; often, they are attracted to models that they view as having power and status and those that they view as kind and nurturing. [■] (C) Features of the task being modeled are another variable that influences attention. [■] (D) Thus teachers will often make use of bright colors, music, or movement as they teach, because these encourage young children to attend to their lessons.

Once the behavior of a model is observed, the input received must be cognitively processed and retained in the form of a general rule. **This general rule** undergoes constant revision based on future observations of others as well as the input received from others regarding the performer's behavior. Production occurs when the observer translates the modeled behavior into **overt** behavior and performs the new behavior. Another subprocess, motivation, plays an important role in production; behaviors viewed as important, ethical, or advantageous to the observer are the ones most often produced.

Bandura's research marked the beginning of a movement toward a view of learning that emphasizes cognitive rather than **behavioral processes**. Social cognitive theory has become one of the major cognitive learning theories dominating the psychological field today.

Now, practice identifying some inference strategies. Determine which inference techniques can be used to find the meanings of the words in bold in the following sentences, then write a synonym or definition for each.

1. Drawing on the animal experiments of Pavlov, who showed how dogs could learn to associate the sound of a bell with food, early behaviorists saw learning as a product of **conditioning**—that is, the repeated performance of an act, usually in the interest of some external reward.

Inference technique: _____

Synonym: _____

Definition: _____

2. During inhibition, the model receives punishment as a consequence for performing a prohibited behavior, and the observer is **discouraged** from performing the behavior. On the other hand, during disinhibition, the prohibited behavior being modeled does not result in a negative consequence for the model, and the observer is encouraged to perform the unacceptable behavior.

Inference technique: _____

Synonym: _____

Definition: _____

3. Behaviorists view learning as a function of environmental factors that promote associations between **stimuli** and responses. Drawing on the animal experiments of Pavlov, who showed how dogs could learn to associate the sound of a bell with food, early behaviorists saw learning as a product of conditioning—that is, the repeated performance of an act, usually in the interest of some external reward.

Inference technique: _____

Synonym: _____

Definition: _____

Answers:

1. *Inference technique.* Identifying synonyms or and explanation in other parts of the passage

   Synonym. Learn to associate [a behavior to a stimulus]

   Definition. The repeated performance of an act, usually in the interest of some external reward.

2. *Inference technique.* Looking for contrasting words or ideas

   Synonym. Prevented

   Definition. To try to prevent by expressing disapproval or raising objections

3. *Inference technique.* Looking for examples

   Synonym. Cause

   Definition. Something that causes a response

Here are some other ways you can determine the defintion of a word.

Look Between Commas

While psychologists tend to agree that learning plays a vital role in human functioning, they have developed very different perspectives, or theories, on its causes, processes, and consequences.

Look Between Dashes

While psychologists tend to agree that learning plays a vital role in human functioning, they have developed very different perspectives—which developed into theories—on its causes, processes, and consequences.

Look After the Verbs *to Be* or *to Mean* or the Phrase *Defined As*

> While psychologists tend to agree that learning plays a vital role in human functioning, they have developed very different perspectives, meaning theories, on its causes, processes, and consequences.

After Phrases Such As *In Other Words* or *In Short*

While psychologists tend to agree that learning plays a vital role in human functioning, they have developed very different perspectives. In other words, many theories try to explain the causes of learning, its processes, and consequences.

Look at the three following sentences from the passage. Rewrite each sentence by adding a definition of the phrase in bold using one of these four ways for presenting definitions.

1. Due to its **pervasive** nature, learning has long been a topic of intense study within psychology.

   _____

2. Modeling is a major construct of the theory and refers to the fact that people learn by observing the behavior of others and the response that the behaviors **elicit** from those around them.

   _____

3. Once the behavior of a model is observed, the input received must be cognitively processed and retained in the form of a general **rule**.

   _____

Answers: Answers will vary. Here are some examples of possible answers.

1. Due to its **pervasive** nature, learning has long been a topic of intense study within psychology. *In other words, learning is a part of almost everything we do, so it is an important focus for psychologists.*

2. Modeling is a major construct of the theory and refers to the fact that people learn by observing the behavior of others and the response that the behaviors **elicit** from, *or bring out of*, those around them.

3. Once the behavior of a model is observed, the input received must be cognitively processed and retained in the form of a general **rule**, *meaning a predictable behavior pattern*.

Now, using the inference strategies you have just practiced, go back to the passage on learning theory and answer the questions that follow.

The word *theories* in the passage is closest in meaning to

- Ⓐ methods
- Ⓑ depths
- Ⓒ perspectives
- Ⓓ treatments

Answer: The sentence in which theories appears is a part of the introduction of the passage. The sentence discusses what psychologists think about learning, stating that they have developed very different perspectives. The key word in the sentence is *or*, which indicates that the writer is introducing a term that has the same meaning as *very different perspectives*. Therefore, answer choice (C) is correct. Choice (A) is a distracter directed at a test taker who doesn't understand that the function of the key word or that *theories* has the same meaning as the phrase that precedes it in the passage. Choice (D) is a distracter directed at a test taker who incorrectly focuses on a connection between *theories* and *psychologists.* Finally, choice (B) refers to the incorrect definition of *perspective*, meaning the technique of representing three-dimensional objects.

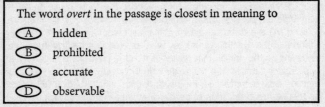

The phrase *get along* in paragraph one is closest in meaning to

(A) travel

(B) succeed

(C) cooperate

(D) be healthy

Answer: In the context of the passage and sentence, the phrase *get along* is closest in meaning to the word *succeed*, choice (B). The paragraph where *get along* appears is about how learning is an important part of life. The sentence lists various essential things that a person must be able to do to function in society. Choice (A) might be attractive to you if you misunderstand *get along* to mean some sort of movement. Choice (C) plays on the meaning of *get along* as working together. However, the main idea of the sentence is related to actions people have to learn, not to people working. Choice (D) would be an attractive distracter if you do not understand the topic of the passage, which is learning. The phrase *be healthy* continues the list of actions that people need to learn but does not have the same meaning as *get along*.

The word *overt* in the passage is closest in meaning to

(A) hidden

(B) prohibited

(C) accurate

(D) observable

Answer: The word that is closest in meaning to *overt* as it is used in the passage is *observable* (D). *Overt* means obvious or not hidden, so the correct answer choice should have a similar meaning. *Observable* means something that can be observed or measured directly. One of the keys to understanding this term is in the beginning of the sentence. The word *production* means that something is being done, in contrast to the sentences earlier in the paragraph that describe how people internalize and process models of behavior. Another key to understanding this term is in the verb *translates*, which means that something is being changed, and the explanatory phrase that follows *overt*: "and performs the new behavior." The context provides clues that *overt behavior* means *open behavior*, and (D) is the choice that is closest in meaning to *open*. None of the other answer choices can be called a synonym of *open*, so they are not as close in meaning to *overt* as *observable* is.

Question Type 7: Locating a Referent

There are three to five passages on the Reading section of the TOEFL. Each passage is generally followed by up to two referent questions.

On the TOEFL, it will not only be necessary for you to determine the meaning of words in a passage but also to locate referents, that is, another word or phrase used to refer to a word. All types of pronouns can be used to refer back to a word, phrase, or idea. Often, as you've already seen, these referents are used to create smooth transitions between sentences. Because many words, phrases, and ideas are usually in a sentence, it can be difficult to locate to which one the pronoun refers. Some techniques that may help you include:

- Eliminating choices that do not correspond in number or gender
- Replacing the pronoun with the choices and checking for meaning or logical words
- Looking for words or phrases with similar grammatical functions

Look at the following sentence from the learning theory passage.

> Drawing on the <u>animal experiments</u> of Pavlov, who showed how dogs could learn to associate the sound of a bell with food, <u>early behaviorists</u> saw <u>learning as a product of conditioning</u>—that is, the repeated performance of an act, usually in the interest of some <u>external reward</u>. **This** led the behaviorists to conclude that learning is essentially the repetition of externally reinforced behaviors.

The pronoun *this* is singular. Therefore, we can automatically eliminate the first two choices, *animal experiments* and *early behaviorists,* which are plural nouns. *External reward* is a singular noun, but
external reward did not lead the behaviorists to formulate a theory of
learning.

> <u>People</u> tend to attend to <u>models</u> and <u>modes</u> of behavior
> that **they** regard as similar to themselves; often, they are
> attracted to models that they view as having <u>power and
> status</u> and those that they view as kind and nurturing.

The pronoun *they* is plural. However, all of the answer choices are
plural, so this fact does not help us eliminate any answer choices.
Fortunately, the two remaining techniques can help us to identify the
correct answer. First, *they* in the second phrase functions as a subject.
The correct answer, *people,* is also the subject of the first phrase in
the sentence. Second, none of the other answer choices is *people.*
Thus, they cannot have a view or opinion of anything.

Now, look at the sentences that follow and circle the word or phrase
to which the underlined pronouns refers. When you are finished,
explain how you determined your answers.

1. While psychologists tend to agree that learning plays a vital
   role in human functioning, <u>they</u> have developed very different
   perspectives, or theories, on its causes, processes, and consequences.

2. Thus, teachers will often make use of bright colors, music, or
   movement as they teach, because <u>these</u> all serve to encourage
   young children to attend to their lessons.

Answers

1. While (psychologists) tend to agree that learning plays a vital
   role in human functioning, <u>they</u> have developed very different
   perspectives, or theories, on its causes, processes, and consequences.

   The sentence begins with the word *while,* which means that the
   sentence will have two clauses divided by a comma. *They* is in
   the subject position of the second part of the sentence, so you

can look to the first part of the sentence to see what *they* refers
to. *Psychologists* is the subject of the first clause, so *they* must
refer to *psychologists*. Another way to look at this question is to
focus on "they have developed different perspectives." None of
the other nouns in the sentence can develop a perspective, so
again, *they* must refer to psychologists.

2. Thus, teachers will often make use of (bright colors, music, or
   movement) as they teach, because <u>these</u> all serve to encourage
   young children to attend to their lessons.

   At first glance, both *teachers* and *bright colors, music, and
   movement* are plural and could be matched with *these*, so
   another strategy, besides matching plural to plural, is necessary
   to answer the question. The key to answering this question
   relies on your understanding of the first part of the sentence,
   "teachers . . . make use of bright colors, music, and movement."
   The second phrase begins with *because,* so it must be an explanation of the reasons teachers use them; therefore, *these*, in
   the subject position of the second phrase, refers to bright colors,
   music, and movement.

Now look again at the passage on the social cognitive theory of learning and answer the questions that follow. Use the referents strategies
you just learned.

The word *its* in the passage refers to

(A) learning

(B) people

(C) nature

(D) psychology

Answer: The possessive pronoun *its* is singular; therefore, its referent must also be singular. Choice (B) is wrong because it is plural.
Choices (C) and (D) are singular but occur in the sentence after
the pronoun *it,* while generally, *it* is used to refer to a noun that has
already been mentioned. (A) is the correct answer.

> The words *This general rule* in the passage refer to:
>
> (A) Received input
>
> (B) Social reactions to a behavior
>
> (C) Important, ethical, or advantageous behavior
>
> (D) Behavior that has been observed and retained

Answer: Choice (D) is correct. A rule is something that governs how people act. Choice (A) is incorrect because it is not a rule. Choice (B) is incorrect because it is not a rule; however, the phrase describes what a person might use to formulate a rule. Choice (C) is incorrect because it does not describe a rule; rather, it describes a type of produced behavior.

Question Type 8: Understanding Coherence

There are three to five passages on the Reading section of the TOEFL. A passage is followed by zero or one coherence question.

You have learned about cohesive devices such as pronouns, demonstrative adjectives, and transitional phrases. These devices are essential to questions on the TOEFL that require you to indicate where a sentence might best fit in the passage.

Review the cognitive theory passage again, found on page 127. Now look at the four sentences that follow and choose a place in the passage you think they might best fit. Explain your answers and list which cohesive devices helped you make your choice.

1. These theories were aptly referred to as "behaviorism."

_____

_____

_____

_____

_____

2. He felt that behaviorism wasn't a complete explanation of how learning occurred.

_____

_____

_____

_____

_____

3. If a teacher wanted to conduct a lesson about simple math, the teacher might use colored blocks and counting songs to keep the children focused on the lesson.

_____

_____

_____

_____

_____

4. Because behaviorism had been so widely accepted, it took many years for the movement to gain widespread popularity.

_____

_____

_____

_____

_____

Answers:

1. These theories were aptly referred to as "behaviorism."

   This sentence is simple and declarative. It needs to be connected to something in the passage that offers an explanation of the theories that formed behaviorism. As the topic of the passage is behaviorism, this sentence likely belongs somewhere in the beginning of the passage, probably near or before where behavior theories are explained. Behavior is discussed for the first time in the second paragraph. The first sentence introduces the behavioral school of psychology, so this sentence belongs immediately after the first sentence of the second paragraph.

2. He felt that behaviorism wasn't a complete explanation of how learning occurred.

   This sentence describes the reason that a person doesn't agree with the theories of behaviorism. Paragraph two explains behaviorism, and so the correct place to insert this sentence is likely shortly after paragraph two. The subject of the sentence is *he*, so the person's name must have already been mentioned; otherwise, the reader would not know to whom the author was referring. Alfred Bandura is introduced in the first sentence of the second paragraph. The third paragraph talks about the process by which Bandura and others challenged behaviorism. The second sentence is about Bandura and his colleagues. *He* is singular, so it wouldn't logically follow the second sentence. Therefore, the best place to put this sentence is in paragraph three, between sentences one and two.

3. If a teacher wanted to conduct a lesson about simple math, the teacher might use colored blocks and counting songs to keep the children focused on the lesson.

   The sentence to be inserted is an example of how a teacher might make use of color and movement to maintain a class' attention to a lesson. The presentation of required content can be adapted to suit a child's preferences. Paragraph six talks about how people adopt certain behavioral models. The sixth sentence is about using bright colors, music, or movement and is grammatically similar to the sentence to be inserted. Therefore the sentence can be inserted after the last sentence of paragraph six.

4. Because behaviorism had been so widely accepted, it took many years for the movement to gain widespread popularity.

This sentence begins with *because* and goes on to refer to a movement. Because of the article *the*, the proper place to insert this sentence must be near an explanation or reference to a movement. The last paragraph of the passage mentions that Bandura's research began a movement toward social cognitive theory, so this sentence can be inserted next.

Using the coherence strategies you have just practiced, answer the following TOEFL questions based once again on "The Social Cognitive Theory of Learning."

Look at the four triangles [▲] that indicate where the following sentence could be added to the passage.

"For example, if a child observes another child often being rewarded with praise for performing a household chore, the first child will learn to associate doing chores with earning praise."

Where would the sentence best fit?

(D)

Answer: Notice the phrase *for example*. When you see an introductory phrase like this, you can often eliminate answer choices. Because the sentence is providing an example, it must follow a statement, usually a new concept or fact in the passage. The sentence after (A) does not introduce anything new to the passage. The sentence after (B) introduces modeling and provides a definition. Inserting the new sentence after (C) might be tempting, but the sentence after (C) continues the explanation of modeling. The sentence after (D) discusses a new topic, research on modeling, so the best place to insert this sentence is after (D).

Look at the four squares [■] that indicate where the following sentence could be added to the passage.

"It is therefore not surprising that for children, parents are among the earliest and most important models. "

Where would the sentence best fit?

(A)

(B)

(C)

(D)

Answer: Choice (A) is incorrect. It is attractive because parents meet the qualifications that the previous sentence describes—they are in a child's daily life and demand a child's attention. However, the next sentence is the first mention of the specific characteristics of a model. Choice (B) is incorrect because it explains the previous sentence by describing the types of models and behaviors to which people tend to be attracted. Choice (C) is correct, because it introduces an example of the type of model that is described in the previous sentences. Choice (D) is incorrect. It states introduces another topic, *features of the task being modeled*. This is not related to who is modeling the behavior.

Now that you have reviewed some reading strategies, let's move on to some writing strategies.

Chapter 10:
Writing: The Persuasive Essay

Recognizing Persuasive Essay Prompts

There are two tasks in the Writing section of the TOEFL. The second is a 30-minute essay based on a single prompt.

One of the essay types that may appear on the TOEFL is the persuasive essay. In a persuasive essay, you will be asked to choose a position on a particular issue and attempt to persuade your audience to agree with the position you've chosen. The structure of a persuasive essay is superficially similar to other essays you may write for the TOEFL; that is, a persuasive essay requires an introduction, body paragraphs, and a conclusion, just like other essays. The difference is that in a persuasive essay, you will not simply be reporting facts; instead, you will be using facts and other information that you have carefully chosen to support your opinion.

Generating Ideas for a Persuasive Essay

Once you have read the prompt carefully and have established that you are being asked to write a persuasive essay, what comes next? What if you have never thought about this topic and have no opinion about it? What strategies can you use to overcome these obstacles and write a great essay? Keep reading to explore several strategies for generating ideas about a topic and formulating those ideas into a well-organized persuasive essay.

Choosing a Point of View

Before you can even start writing, you must decide which point of view you will support in your essay. Your best choice will probably be the position that is easiest to defend, not necessarily the one that you personally agree with. On the TOEFL, you have a limited amount of time, so it is important to make the most of what you have.

Before you decide which position to support, carefully consider both sides of the issue. Once you have done this, choosing a position may be a great deal easier. One helpful strategy is to make a list of all the ideas you have about the topic. What facts and arguments favor side A? What information and arguments, on the other hand, support side B? After you have completed the list, it will be much easier to see which position is the strongest and the easiest to support in your essay.

An alternative to listing is freewriting. Remember from Chapter 2 on writing that when freewriting, you write continuously for several minutes, writing down every idea or thought about the topic that comes into your mind. Again, when you have finished freewriting, the relative strengths of the possible positions on the topic should be clearer, and you will be able to choose the best one to support in your essay.

Look at the following prompts. Choose the prompt that seems the most interesting to you.

- Recently, several nations have begun seriously discussing a manned mission to Mars. Do you think that such exploration is a worthwhile endeavor? Explain why or why not.
- Many people feel that the national government has a responsibility to provide support for its citizens who are too old to work. Do you agree that governments are responsible for taking care of retired citizens? Why or why not? Provide reasons and details in your response.
- In your opinion, which is more important, family or work? Provide examples and details to support your answer.

After choosing one of the above prompts, carefully consider all sides of the issue it discusses and make a note of each idea, argument, or fact you can think of related to this issue. List them in the following chart:

Side A	Side B

Sample Responses: Responses will vary, but here is one example based on the prompt about Mars exploration.

Side A: SHOULD Go to Mars	Side B: SHOULDN'T Go to Mars
Many useful technologies were developed by other space programs—plastics, fuels, medicines.	The cost of traveling to the Moon was very high, so going to Mars will be even more expensive because it is farther away.
If an entire nation or society gets behind a project, it can boost morale, give people hope, and encourage kids to study the sciences.	Given the problems with space travel over the last 20 years, it seems that we do not have the technology to build a very safe spacecraft.
Humans can react faster and make their own decisions without waiting for instructions. A manned mission would be much more capable and adaptable than a robotic mission.	Robots can do most of the jobs that a person could. But they would require fewer resources, and they would be lower risk.

Outlining a Persuasive Essay

Once you've brainstormed the topic, chosen your position, written your thesis statement, and decided which arguments to use to support your position, you're ready for the next step in preparing your essay: organizing it. Before you begin to write your essay, you should have a clear idea how you will present your ideas. An excellent technique to help you with this is to prepare an outline.

Remember, it is not essential that the outline be extensively detailed. It should contain enough information to keep you on track but not so much that writing it cuts into the time you need for writing the essay itself.

Here is a model outline for a persuasive essay.

I. Introductory paragraph
   A. Hook: a device for capturing reader's attention
   B. Background information: to help reader understand topic
   C. Thesis statement: clear statement of your position
II. First supporting argument: strong reason supporting your position
   A. Topic sentence: general factual sentence introducing paragraph
   B. Facts, examples, arguments to support and prove argument
III. Second supporting argument (as in II)
   A. Topic sentence
   B. Facts, examples, arguments
IV. Third supporting argument (as in II and III)
   A. Topic sentence
   B. Facts, examples, arguments
V. Conclusion
   A. Reviews important points from the discussion
   B. Clearly states what lesson or message should be taken from the essay

Writing the Introduction to a Persuasive Essay

The introduction of a persuasive essay has a more important role than any other part of the essay. It should do four things:

1. **Attract the reader's attention as quickly as possible, ideally within the first sentence or two.** This is called a hook. (Remember this from Chapter 2 about writing?) A good hook can take many forms: an anecdote; a provocative rhetorical question (a question directed to the reader); an interesting fact; or a strong, clearly opinionated claim about the topic.

2. **Provide useful background information about the essay's topic.** Carefully choose information that reflects your point of view in a positive way. If you intend to propose and support a position, you will want to present the information or conditions that clearly demonstrate that some decision or course of action is necessary. (Later, in the body, you will demonstrate that the

opinion or course of action you are recommending is the best one.) Be sure to provide enough background information for your reader to understand the topic.

3. **Make clear to the reader what feelings you have on the topic. Your opinion or recommendation must be clearly stated.** The best way to do this is with a thesis statement, a strongly worded statement of your position on the topic. Generally, this will be the last sentence of the introduction.

4. **Refer to the main arguments you intend to mention in the essay to support your position.** List these arguments in the same order you will be presenting them in the body. This forecasting will help your reader understand how your essay is organized and how your arguments will be constructed. Forecasting is either done within the thesis statement or in another sentence immediately following the thesis.

Here is a summary of what the introductory paragraph of a persuasive essay should include:

- A hook, to attract the reader's attention
- Background information, to set the stage for your discussion
- A thesis statement, which clearly states your opinion or recommendation
- Forecasting, a brief listing of all the main arguments your essay will discuss

Read the introduction to the model essay, "Homeschooling." After the essay, describe how this introduction does or does not accomplish the four essential tasks of a persuasive essay introduction.

Homeschooling (introduction)

American parents today are faced with a stark choice. The country's public schools are becoming more crowded, more violent, and less effective in preparing children for employment or college. Private schools may be too expensive or unavailable. To ensure that their children receive an adequate education, an increasing number of parents are simply teaching their children at home. While home-

schooling offers many benefits to both child and parent,
its three most important advantages are its flexibility of
curriculum, its adaptability to different learning styles and
speeds, and its more positive, supportive social environment.

_____
_____
_____
_____
_____
_____
_____
_____
_____
_____
_____
_____
_____
_____
_____
_____
_____
_____
_____
_____
_____
_____
_____
_____

Sample Answers: Answers will vary slightly, but here are some examples:

- **Hook.** Parents are faced with a stark choice.
- **Background.** Public schools are too crowded and less effective, private schools too expensive.
- **Thesis statement.** Homeschooling offers many benefits to child and parent.
- **Forecasting.** Advantages are flexibility, adaptability, and supportive social environment.

Writing Thesis Statements and Topic Sentences for a Persuasive Essay

The thesis statement of a persuasive essay is different from those you may write in some other essay types in one important way: it must be a firm statement of opinion, not simply a fact. It must reflect the judgment you have made about the topic and must identify the point of view or recommendation you are putting forward for the reader's consideration. The rest of the essay will be devoted to defending this opinion.

Remember, when you are writing a persuasive essay on the TOEFL, choose the point of view that is easiest for you to defend with the information you have available. This might not be the position you personally favor. Without solid arguments to support your thesis, you cannot write a persuasive essay. It is also important to remember that there is no right or wrong position on any TOEFL essay question. The essay graders are only interested in how well you can present and defend your opinion, not which side you choose.

A good way to write your thesis statement is to read the original question or claim closely, then carefully paraphrase it in a new sentence that also expresses the opinion you have about that question or claim. Remember, to paraphrase is to rewrite the original idea in your own words, without changing the meaning.

Let's consider an example. Suppose you are given the following prompt:

> Do you agree that schools should make daily exercise a part of their curriculum? Explain why or why not.

In response, you could write a thesis statement like one of the following:

- I feel strongly that regular exercise should be a component of any child's education for the following reasons: exercise reduces stress, prevents weight gain, and improves academic performance.

- Because habitual exercise reduces stress, prevents weight gain, and improves academic performance, exercise should be made a part of any school's curriculum.

A carefully written thesis statement offers three benefits. First, and most importantly, a thesis statement will help prevent you from accidentally wandering from the precise topic the prompt is asking you to address; straying from the topic could lead to a substantial reduction in your essay's score. Second, a good thesis statement will clearly tell the reader where you stand on the issue and how you will defend that position in the body of the essay. Third, good paraphrasing will give you an opportunity to demonstrate your knowledge of English.

THE BODY OF A PERSUASIVE ESSAY

Writing Topic Sentences

Each body paragraph of your persuasive essay should begin with a sentence that clearly identifies the argument that paragraph will make in support of the essay's thesis: its topic sentence. You may remember the discussion of the topic sentence in Chapter 6 on writing. If not, a brief review follows.

A topic sentence should work like a good umbrella: it should cover everything found underneath it. That is, the topic sentence should be general enough to include all the information you wish to include in that paragraph. By the same token, the paragraph should include no information that is outside the general topic introduced by the topic sentence.

Another important feature of a good topic sentence is the transition words or phrases that indicate the progression of ideas in your essay and the logical connections between them. There are several ways you can do this. Using words like *first, second,* or *finally* tells your reader that you are leaving one idea and going on to the next. Words like *moreover* and *furthermore* tell your reader that you are about to make another point that is connected to the previous topic. Phrases and words like *on the other hand, however,* and *in contrast* tell the reader that you are about to discuss an idea that contrasts with or opposes the previous idea.

Read the body of the essay on homeschooling. Pay close attention to the topic sentence of each paragraph and consider the questions that follow.

Homeschooling (body)

First, a curriculum designed around the interests of a particular child is an enormous asset in education. If, for example, the child is interested in dinosaurs, that subject could be used to teach scientific concepts from geology, biology, or even history. Moreover, in the home environment, there is plenty of room for spontaneous discussion, impromptu field trips, and other learning experiences that classroom logistics make difficult, expensive, or challenging. Homeschooling puts the child's natural curiosity to use, limited only by the imagination of the child and parent.

Furthermore, the home classroom adapts to individual learning styles. Children can move through the material at a rate that challenges them positively. In the conventional classroom, most lessons are aimed at the middle level of ability. Thus, some students are dragged along much faster than is optimal for them, while others yawn or find distractions. Nor can a teacher pay much attention to any single student in a classroom of 30 or discover how individual students learn best. But the parent at home, who knows the child better than any teacher, can readily make adjustments to content, teaching strategy, or pace, as the child requires.

The final important advantage of homeschooling lies in the socialization children can receive. Homeschooled children are less subject to the stresses and pressures experienced by conventional students who spend six, seven, or eight hours a day with their peers. They are less likely to become involved with gangs or drugs. On the other hand, homeschooled children spend much more time in the company of appropriate role models: parents, other adults, and older siblings. In this environment, they are better able to learn from actual life situations and to learn how to interact with people of all ages. In particular, homeschooling fosters healthy family relationships, because both children and their parents can play larger and more complete roles in one another's lives.

Though there are important advantages to homeschooling, there are also certain disadvantages, which a parent who is considering this option should take into account. The first of these is simply a practical one. If both parents work out of the home, care must be found for young children while the parents are away. Indeed, working parents may be unable to find the time to provide schooling for their children at all, and hiring a tutor to fill that role is an expensive proposition. Second, parents may be attacked for choosing what many people feel is an anti-social or elitist option—for thinking that their children are better than anyone else's, for refusing to participate in an important social institution, or even for trying to destroy public schools by depriving them of students and funding. Third, not all parents will be comfortable in the role of teacher. They may not have the patience required, the basic knowledge of the material, or the energy to encourage and motivate their children when necessary.

Homeschooling is not a panacea for the institutional deficiencies found in American public schools; these can only be addressed through a large-scale restructuring of public education policies nationwide. Nevertheless, homeschooling offers a number of significant advantages to parents and children. And it works. Homeschooled children, on average, place in the 87th percentile on standardized exams—the national average is the 50th percentile—and have been admitted to all major universities and military academies in the country. Clearly, homeschooling is a serious, positive alternative for motivated parents and their children.

1. Is each topic sentence general enough to include all the ideas and information discussed in the paragraph?

_____

_____

2. What kind of transition words or phrases does each paragraph use?

_____

_____

3. Would you make any changes to these topic sentences?

_____

_____

Answers:

1. Yes

2. First, Furthermore, The final, Though, Nevertheless

3. Answers will vary.

The Body of a Persuasive Essay

Once you have brainstormed the topic and written your thesis state-ment, decide exactly what information you will include in the body of the essay to support and defend the thesis.

A good persuasive essay will have at least two well-developed body paragraphs. Three is better. Each paragraph will discuss a particular aspect of the topic and contain both a general topic sentence and several sentences containing information and examples that support the topic sentence.

Earlier in this chapter we saw this sample thesis statement:

> Because habitual exercise reduces stress, prevents weight gain, and improves academic performance, exercise should be made a part of any school's curriculum.

This sentence mentions three subtopics that can be used to argue in favor of the thesis: stress reduction, weight gain prevention, and improved academic performance. Each of these subtopics will be turned into the topic sentence of a body paragraph; each may also contain a transition word that shows where it belongs in the overall essay structure. Here are three examples showing how this could be done:

1. First, habitual exercise is a great outlet for the stress that many students feel in the academic environment.

2. Moreover, regular exercise has been shown to be more effective than any diet in preventing excessive weight gain and all the ill-nesses associated with being overweight.

3. Most importantly, students who exercise regularly display supe-rior academic performance.

When you are ready, use the skills and strategies you have learned in this chapter to complete the following essay practice.

PRACTICE: ESSAY WRITING

Following is an example of the second task in the Writing section of the TOEFL. Read the question that follows. You have 30 minutes to plan, write, and revise your essay. Typically, an effective response will contain a minimum of 300 words.

> A major corporation is considering making a very large donation. Two charities are being considered: the first is a worldwide rainforest preservation fund; the second supports after-school mentoring and activities for local elementary school children. Which charity do you think should receive the donation? Provide reasons and examples in your response.

_____

_____

_____

_____

_____

_____

_____

_____

_____

_____

_____

_____

_____

_____

_____

Answer: Answers will vary, but here is one sample essay.

Sample Essay: A Large Donation

Both the decline of the world's rainforests and the need for educational opportunity for children are important issues. While the problem of the rainforests needs to be addressed, many resources are already being devoted to this problem. On the other hand, students today are faced with overwhelming challenges as they learn, and often many parents must work to support their families. Because many families lack the resources and time to focus on a child's education, it is important that more adults become involved with the children in a community and that children have opportunities to learn outside of a classroom. However, without financial support, mentoring and other after-school programs are very difficult to maintain.

It is also important for companies to invest locally. Companies should support the communities that surround them for several reasons. First, it is likely that some of the employees have or know children in the affected schools. Providing support to those schools would help to build morale and the reputation of the company in the community. Second, a company that is involved with education is investing in itself. If people view the company as a part of their community, then it is likely that some children in the community will want to work for the company later, when they are older and have families of their own.

Supporting children with mentors and after-school programs will give them opportunities and guidance that they might not receive otherwise. Problems like class size and lack of resources are common in many schools, so some children do not get the attention that they need. Extending the amount of time that kids have to learn helps ensure that they don't miss out. For example, if a first grader is having trouble learning to read, a teacher might not have time to sit with that child during the regular school day. However, a well-trained after-school volunteer could work with the child in a one-on-one or small group situation to help them learn better.

Finally, investing in education is a wise long-term investment for everyone. Students who are better educated will be better able to solve problems—like the decline of rainforests. Making donations to enhance the education of children in a community is one of the best investments a company can make.

When you are ready, move on to the next chapter.

Chapter 11:
Listening: Taking Notes
from a Conversation

Turns

In an essay, the main element of organization is the paragraph; in conversation it is called the turn. A turn is a statement or question and the response that follows. These go together to form a coherent unit—they relate to the same idea. As you see in the following conversation, a turn can be a question and direct response:

Sarah: What time does the concert start tomorrow?

Mike: About 8:00.

However, a turn can extend over several statements and responses, as you see in the following conversation:

Sarah: What time does the concert start tomorrow?

Mike: Which one, the jazz concert or the '60s show in the park?

Sarah: The '60s concert.

Mike: Oh, are you going to go?

Sarah: Sure. Do you want to come?

Mike: That would be great. It's not going to be very crowded, so why don't we get there just before 8:00?

In this example, the response to Sarah's question about what time the concert begins is not answered directly. The actual response to this question comes after several statements and questions between Mike and Sarah. You may also notice that Mike's response in the second conversation is not as direct as in the first. In the second conversation, he answers Sarah's direct question with an indirect question: "Why don't we get there just before 8:00?"

You can see that the structure of a conversation can be very complex. On the TOEFL, you will answer questions based on conversations that involve numerous turns, as well as on lectures that include student comments and questions in turns with what the professor is saying.

PRACTICE: LISTENING QUESTIONS

There are several different question types on the Listening section of the TOEFL. Chapters 3 and 7 covered the following types:

- Understanding Rhetorical Function
- Drawing an Inference
- Understanding a Speaker's Implication

This chapter will cover three more question types:

- Identifying the Main Idea
- Summarizing the Most Important Points
- Understanding Details

Question Type 4—Identifying the Main Idea

There are two or three conversations and four to six lectures in the Listening section of the TOEFL.

Main idea questions ask you to consider the entire lecture. While listening to the lecture, you should do the following things in order to identify the main idea:

- Listen carefully to the short introductory statement at the beginning of each lecture for key information about the context or topic.
- Understand how the speaker feels about the ideas he or she is presenting.

Wrong answers relate to points in the lecture, but they do not summarize the lecture well. Distracters may either summarize one portion of the lecture but not the whole lecture, and thus are too narrow, or they may be too broad given the specific focus of the lecture.

Common stems for this kind of question are as follows:

- This talk is mainly about…
- The professor is mainly discussing…
- What is the main topic/idea of the lecture?

You may refer to your notes when answering all listening questions. In the listening questions, the question and the answer choices appear on the computer screen, but only the question is spoken by the narrator.

Here is a main idea question based on the "public art" discussion transcribed here.

Narrator: Listen to part of a talk in an art history class.

Professor (female): Okay, let's get started. Today, we're going to continue our discussion by talking about public art. Who can sum up the textbook's definition of public art for the class?

Student A (male): I think the book says that it's, ah, it's basically any work of art that's readily available to the general population—it's either mounted in an outdoor space, or in a building that's accessible to the public.

Professor: So by that definition, wouldn't an exhibit at a museum be public art, because the building is somewhat open to the public? Or is there more to it than that?

Student A: No…it doesn't really apply to art that can be found in museums or galleries. It's more like art that uses the public space as part of the exhibit. One of the examples in the book was Michelangelo's painting on the ceiling of the Sistine Chapel. [pauses] I guess it sort of applies to buildings where you wouldn't expect to see art…like in churches, or Keith Haring's graffiti in New York City's subways…

Professor: That's it. You hit it right on the head. The distinction between public art and most other forms of art is that public art turns up in places where it's least expected—painted church ceilings, statues in parks, subway graffiti... [trailing off].

Does anyone remember the Cow Parade exhibit we had in the city a few summers ago? I see some of you shaking your heads. Well, during Cow Parade, there were about 250 life-size cows made out of plaster that were on exhibit throughout the city. Local artists had the opportunity to purchase a cow, decorate it in any way they wanted to, and exhibit it on the streets of the city. Each individual cow had a theme, and the cows were put up on streets all throughout Manhattan for a few months. During that time, anyone and everyone had access to the cows. In my opinion, Cow Parade is a great example of public art, as well as one of the most exciting and innovative ideas I've seen recently.

Okay...so we've established that public art is a piece of art that uses its surroundings and is readily available to the public. There's more information on that topic in last night's reading so we won't review it now. But what else is distinctive about public art?

Student B (female): Well, artists can put up works outside, and use that space to create big works of art that would never fit in a gallery...like when Christo and Jeanne-Claude put up The Gates in Central Park. They hung that saffron-colored material from big doorways—or gates—along 23 miles of the park, and tons of people went to the park to see them. The whole point was that the sunlight would hit the material and it would billow in the wind and it would be beautiful. They could never have found an indoor space that would have created the same effect.

Professor: I'm glad you brought that up. The Gates exhibit is a good example, because it exemplifies a lot of the elements of public art. Something we've already discussed is how public art takes the natural surroundings into account, and works with them. Do you guys know that it took over 20 years for the Gates to be approved by New York City, in part because the artists needed to find a way to build the gates without any adverse impact on the environment? That was one of the stipulations of the artists' contract with the City, and they couldn't move the project forward until they solved that dilemma.

Just like The Gates, much of the public art we see is controversial. Many people wonder, is it really [emphasis] art to drape a million square yards of fabric across poles in Central Park? Is it really [emphasis] art to spray-paint figures on subway station billboards? Or to paint a couple of plaster cows and park them on street corners in New York City? Or does art need to be more cultured, more refined, more thoughtful than that? We'll get into that discussion a little later, though.

So now we've mentioned a few of the factors that need to be present for a work to be called public art. The work has to be fully, and easily, available to the public, either on display outdoors or in an accessible building. The piece should have a synergistic relationship with its surroundings, and it's usually contemporary. Okay, let's go to our books and see what some of our more well-known critics have to say about this subject.

What is the lecture mainly about?

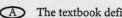 The textbook definition of art in outdoor spaces

Ⓑ Art that is intended to be viewed in public spaces

Ⓒ An overview of how art is viewed by the public

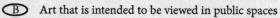 How the Sistine Chapel and subway graffiti are connected

Answer

Choice (A) is too narrow, and it is mentioned in the introduction to define the term "public art." Choice (C) may be a tempting answer because art is a keyword in the lecture that is frequently repeated; however, this answer is too broad because it fails to place art in the context of public venues. Choice (D) presents only two examples of public art and is therefore too narrow in scope. Choice (B) is correct.

Question Type 5—Summarizing the Most Important Points

There are two or three conversations and four to six lectures in the Listening section of the TOEFL.

This type of TOEFL question asks you to identify the three most important points in the lecture, the points that combine to express the main idea. The incorrect options either provide points that don't support the main idea or points that are inaccurate. This question can be presented in two distinct formats:

- Choose three out of five options—the first sample question
- Click on yes or no for each of five options—the second sample question

As in all listening questions, the question and the answer choices appear on the screen, but only the question is spoken by the narrator

According to the lecture, which of the following would be considered examples of public art?

Click on three answers.

(A) A sculpture in a private garden

(B) Large chalk sketches on a sidewalk

(C) A series of statues exhibited throughout the streets of a city

(D) A museum exhibit of images of large crowds

(E) Animal sculptures that make up a children's playground

Answer

Choice (A) is not an example of public art, according to the lecture, because public art must be available to the general population. Choice (D) is clearly expressed by one of the students as not public art, because when the professor asks about art in museums, the student explains that public art somehow makes use of its surroundings. The professor then implies that art in museums and galleries is not public art because it is expected to be there. Choices (B), (C), and (E) are all correct. Choice (B) is similar to graffiti, which was mentioned in the talk. Choice (C) is describing the Cow Parade in New York. Choice (E) is also correct because the professor mentions that public art should "have a synergistic relationship with its surroundings."

In the lecture, the professor talks about how public art is
defined. Indicate whether she mentions the following as
factors of public art.

Click in the correct box for each phrase.

	Yes	No
(A) It has a synergistic connection to its surroundings.	☐	☐
(B) It is displayed in multiple galleries	☐	☐
(C) It is most often antique or historical	☐	☐
(D) It often appears in unexpected places	☐	☐
(E) It is available to the general population	☐	☐

The professor explicitly states public art has a synergistic relationship
to its surroundings, so choice (A) is *yes*. The professor asks whether
art in museums and galleries can be considered public, but she later
implies that art that appears in predictable places is not considered
public art, so (B) is *no*. She mentions Michelangelo's work in the
Sistine Chapel, but later states that public art is "usually contemporary" so (C) is *no*. She says that public art "turns up in spaces where
it's least expected," so (D) is *yes*. The professor also states several
times that public art is by definition accessible to the general public,
so (E) is *yes*.

Question Type 6—Understanding Details

There are two or three conversations and four to six lectures in the
Listening section of the TOEFL.

Detail questions will require you to recall specific information from the
spoken text. The answer choices will contain three inaccurate statements and one right one.

To answer direct information questions, you should do the following as you take notes:

- Listen carefully to the conversation.
- Try to understand unfamiliar words from context.
- Pay special attention to numbers and proper nouns.

The most common stem for this type of question is:

- According to _____ , who/what/when/where/why/how many/how much...?

You will be able to use your notes when you answer detail questions. Remember that on the listening questions, both the questions and the answer choices will appear on the screen, but only the question will be spoken.

Here is an example of a detail question.

According to the professor, where can public art be found?

(A) Museums

(B) Shopping malls

(C) Galleries

(D) Churches

Answer

Choice (A) mentioned as a place where art is NOT considered public. Choice (B) is an arbitrary location that has no relation to the lecture. Choice (C) is also mentioned as a place where the pieces on display are not considered to be "public art." Choice (D) is the correct answer. The professor explicitly states that public art can appear on church ceilings.

On some detail questions you will be instructed to click on more than one correct answer, as shown here.

Which of the following would the professor most likely agaree with as examples of public art?

Click on 2 answers.

(A) A showroom of famous portraits

(B) A garden maze in a park

(C) A mural of a town's habitation

(D) A photography exhibit

Answer

Choice (A) is incorrect because the speaker clearly states that public art appears where it is not expected. Choice (B) is correct because it is a type of sculpture that has a relationship with its surroundings. Choice (C) also takes its setting into consideration, so it is also correct. Choice (D) is incorrect because the speaker implies that exhibits are expected to present works of art, and therefore are not public.

A variation of the detail question is one in which you need to choose the answer that is NOT true. These questions take the following format:

- Which of the following is/is NOT…?
- All of the following… EXCEPT…

Try this variation on the detail question:

All of the following are mentioned as public art EXCEPT

(A) A gallery of famous paintings

(B) Graffiti on a subway

(C) The Cow

(D) The ceiling of the Sistine Chapel

Answer

Choices (B), (C), and (D) are mentioned in the lecture as examples of public art, so you should NOT choose any of these choices. You should choose (A) because, galleries were specifically mentioned as NOT places where public art can be found.

When you are ready, begin Speaking Chapter 12: Summarizing and Synthesizing.

Chapter 12:
Speaking: Summarizing and Synthesizing

Remember that in Chapters 4 and 8, we covered the following speaking tasks:

- Describing something from your own experience
- Summarizing a lecture
- Expressing and supporting an opinion based on personal experience
- Summarizing a conversation and expressing an opinion

This chapter covers one more speaking task:

- Synthesizing and summarizing information

Before we review this task, let's cover some other important skills and strategies.

Informal versus Formal Speech

In English, there are many ways of saying the same thing. A speaker or writer chooses particular words and expressions depending on their goal and who makes up their audience. For example, you probably wouldn't speak to a professor in the same way you would speak to your best friend. You probably would speak more formally to your professor than to your friend.

Listen to these two statements of opinion. Think about what language is formal and what language is informal. If you have a study partner, or someone who can listen to your response, ask that person to read the following transcript.

⊞ Informal versus Formal Practice: The Environment

I think that we've gotta protect the environment really soon, or we'll be in a lot of trouble. It's stupid when companies decide not to follow simple rules that are supposed to cut down the tons of trash that people make every day. I mean stuff like recycling and using less electricity, you know, like turning down the A/C in buildings in the summer, and lowering the heat when it's cold out. But nobody wants to do that, 'cuz they don't want to be too cold or too hot. If we don't start following the laws—I mean making less trash and using less power—I think that the whole planet's gonna be in really big trouble soon.

I think that protecting the environment is crucial. It seems foolish that many companies choose not to follow the basic environmental regulations that govern recycling and reduce the amount of electricity we use every day. For instance, turning down air-conditioning during the summer and lowering heating systems in the winter might reduce the amount of energy used, but people are reluctant to do so because they don't want to be uncomfortable. We may enjoy our comfort now, but if we don't begin to enforce environmental laws soon, we will have to confront our waste problems in the near future, or the entire planet may have to deal with the consequences.

Now make a note of words and phrases from the statements that have the same meaning but different tone. Write them in the correct columns. An example has been filled in for you.

Informal	Formal	Either Informal or Formal
laws	regulations	rules

Possible answers:

Informal/ Conversational	Formal	Either Informal or Formal
laws	regulations	rules
rules	foolish	
stupid	reduce	
cut down	air-conditioning	air-conditioning
A/C	energy	electricity
power	waste	
trash	heating systems	temperature
heat	uncomfortable	
too cold or too hot		

Gliding

What is gliding? Gliding is one way that English speakers link particular words together. They tend to pronounce words in thought groups rather than individually. There are no pauses between these words.

Here is an example:

- from an early age

If one word ends in a vowel sound *(early)* and the next word begins with a vowel sound *(age)*, how is it possible to link them without pausing? That's where gliding comes in. A kind of consonant called a glide is added between the two vowels when the words are spoken: from an early[y]age.

The consonant that is added is either a *y* sound or a *w* sound, depending on the last vowel sound of the first word. Don't worry about this detail now. Just think about where a glide may occur.

Look at the following sentences and draw a line connecting two words that would probably be pronounced with an added glide. The first one has been done for you as an example.

1. Those two are always talking about the effects of exercise!

2. Do you know why it's so important?

3. Apparently exercise aids learning.

4. It's only two in the afternoon.

5. I'll be in the library if you need me.

6. I'll probably go on Friday.

7. Maybe it's better to rely on hard science.

8. Scientists need to invest more time on the issue in the future.

9. Basically, I think this should be essential to instruction from now on.

10. Let's do it soon; we only have one more day to finish it.

Answers:

1. Those two are always talking about the effects of exercise!

2. Do you know why it's so important?

3. Apparently exercise aids learning.

4. It's only two in the afternoon.

5. I'll be in the library if you need me.

6. I'll probably go on Friday.

7. Maybe it's better to rely on hard science.

8. Scientists need to invest more time on the issue in the future.

9. Basically, I think this should be essential to instruction from now on.

10. Let's do it soon; we only have one more day to finish it.

PRACTICE: SPEAKING TASKS

There are six tasks in the Speaking section of the TOEFL. The third requires you to read an announcement, listen to a conversation about the announcement, and answer a question that asks you to synthesize and summarize information from both the announcement you read and the conversation you heard. You have 30 seconds to prepare your response, and your response should be about 60 seconds in length.

When reading the notice and listening to the conversation you should:

- Identify the main points
- Identify the main speaker's opinion and the reasons the speaker holds that opinion

Task 3: Synthesizing and Summarizing Information

Listen to the narrator's introduction. Remember that you will not see the narrator's introduction to the question on the test. If you have a study partner, or someone who can listen to your response, ask that person to read the transcript while you take notes.

Narrator: In this question, you will read a short text and then listen to a dialog about the same topic. You will hear a question about what you have read and heard. You will then have 30 seconds to prepare your response and 60 seconds to speak.

Eastern State University is planning to change its parking policy. Read the announcement about the change from the Department of Public Safety. You will have 45 seconds to read the announcement. Begin reading now.

Now read the announcement below, and have a partner read out loud the following Discussion and Prompt transcripts.

An Announcement from the Department of Public Safety

Eastern State University has announced a new parking policy, which will go into effect in September 2007. This policy is intended to ensure that the very limited number of parking spaces available on campus are allocated as fairly as possible. Up to now, preference was given to faculty and staff and then to commuting students. Any remaining parking spaces were offered to students living on campus on the basis of seniority. Beginning with the coming academic year, the university will give out parking spaces by means of a lottery. Details about the lottery are available on the DPS Web site.

Discussion: Public Safety Announcement

Narrator: Listen to two students as they discuss the change in policy.

Student A (female): Why is it that the commuters are always getting discriminated against?

Student B (male): I think the new system's a good idea. At least everyone'll have a fair shot. The faculty won't get special treatment.

Student A: It's the commuters who deserve special treatment. Most of the professors live pretty close by. For those of us who live far away from campus, convenience is a necessity. Now, we'll have to waste precious study time driving around in circles. Or worse yet, we'll have to pay some garage.

Student B: You can't really say we don't get special treatment. The annual fee we pay for a permit's a lot lower than what the faculty pays.

Student A: At least, under the old system, we were guaranteed spots till they ran out. Now, I'll be competing with everyone . . . including people who live on campus. Under this new policy, I'll just have to hope I get lucky.

Student B: You know, my brother's school instituted a similar system last year. For some reason, a lot of people didn't even bother entering. So who knows? Maybe we'll actually have a better chance than before . . . .

Student A expressed an opinion about a new university policy. State that student's opinion and explain the reasons the student gave for holding that opinion.

| 30 seconds to prepare | 60 seconds to speak. |

Now evaluate yourself using the following criteria:

Criteria	Comments	Action to Improve
Clarity and pronunciation		
Organization		
Details and examples		
Grammar and vocabulary		

Now ask your partner to read the sample response from the following transcript. How is it different from yours? How is it similar?

(🔊) **Sample Response: Public Safety Announcement**

The student feels that the new lottery doesn't treat students who commute to school fairly. The school used to handle parking by guaranteeing spots to commuter students until the spots ran out. The new system will assign students parking spaces through a lottery system. Commuting students do not have priority anymore. The student says that this new system isn't fair, because commuting students live farther away than faculty and they shouldn't have to compete for space with students who already live on campus. The student also says that commuters will have to spend time searching for parking, which will take away from study time.

Following is some more practice on this particular TOEFL speaking task: *synthesizing and summarizing information*. To review, this task requires you to read a notice and listen to a short conversation about the information presented in the notice. You will be able to take notes both as you read and as you listen. You will have 30 seconds to prepare a 60-second response in which you summarize the speaker's opinion about the notice and give reasons why the speaker holds that opinion.

If you have a study partner, or someone who can listen to your response, ask that person to read the following transcript.

Narrator: In this question, you will read a notice and listen to a conversation on the same topic. You will then answer a question about the notice and conversation. After you hear the question, you will have 30 seconds to prepare your response and 60 seconds to speak.

North Park University is planning to build new athletic facilities. Read the announcement about the plans from the Office of Alumni Relations. You will have 45 seconds to read the announcement. Begin reading now.

Now read the following announcement to yourself and have a friend read the subsequent discussion transcript and prompt out loud.

An Announcement from the Office of Alumni Relations

North Park University is pleased to announce that construction of a new sports facility will commence this spring. Among the features of the new state-of-the-art sports complex will be a basketball court and an Olympic-size swimming pool. The new center, which will be used for competitions as well as for recreation, is made possible by a generous grant from Thomas C. Watson, a 1969 alumnus of the university. It is thanks to the generous support of alumni like Mr. Watson that we can make

---

🔘 **Discussion: Alumni Relations Announcement**

Narrator: Listen to two students as they discuss the announcement.

Student A: Why is it that the athletes always get all the money? It's so unfair!

Student B: Have you *w* the swimming pool we have now? Can you believe we've had the same pool since 1904?

Student A: And can you believe I live in the only dorm on campus that doesn't have Internet access? And that the bio labs haven't been renovated since my dad was a student here? I have nothing against sports. I'm only saying that the university should spend its limited resources in ways that'll do the most good for the largest number of people.

Student B: Athletics are important. They help students relieve stress and keep their bodies in good shape. And our sports teams help foster school spirit.

Student A: That's all very nice, but I just think the administration has its priorities all wrong. They should put academics first. Talk about stress! I could use a new language lab to improve my grades. That'd help *my* stress.

Student B: Look at the bright side. Maybe our fancy new sports center will will earn so much money in ticket sales that they'll be able to add several labs.

Student A expresses an opinion about the announcement made by the alumni office. State Student A's opinion and explain the reasons Student A gives for holding that opinion.

30 seconds to prepare   60 seconds to speak.

Now evaluate yourself using the following criteria:

Criteria	Comments	Action to Improve
Clarity and pronunciation		
Organization		
Details and examples		
Grammar and vocabulary		

Now listen to the sample response. How is it different from yours? How is it similar?

🔊 Sample Response: Alumni Relations Announcement

Student A doesn't like the idea of a new swimming pool. This student points out that their dorm doesn't have Internet access and that the biology labs have not been renovated for a long time. Student A thinks that the university needs to focus on things that will benefit the most students, like academics and classrooms and things like that. If the money goes to the new pool, Student A says that it will only help people who use the pool regularly, like athletes, who are a small group at the school.

Great work! You are now one chapter closer to completing this book. If you are ready, turn to Part 4 for the final set of reading, writing, listening, and speaking chapters.

Part Five
Synthesis and Review

Part Five covers more reading, writing, listening, and speaking skills and strategies you will need to score high on the TOEFL, while continuing to build upon what you have learned in previous chapters. To get the most out of this part, make sure to complete all the practice exercises and sample questions.

Chapter 13:
Reading: Context

More about Transitions

Recall from Chapter 9 on reading that transitional words and phrases can help the reader identify which type of text an author has written. For example, words and phrases such as the following might point to a compare/contrast passage:

- Unlike
- Compared to
- On the other hand
- Likewise
- Similarly

These words and phrases, however, might indicate a persuasive, argumentative type of text:

- Offers a number of advantages
- Some benefits include
- An additional reason is

Summarizing Two Sources

You have learned that both the ability to summarize and the ability to paraphrase from lectures, texts, and conversations are essential skills for students at an American university. In this chapter, you will practice these skills again to synthesize, or combine, the information from a text and a lecture.

Read the following passage.

The Real Estate Boom

The recent real estate boom in the United States seems to have overtaken the stock market as the preferred method of investment. The median price of a home in the United States has gone up over 55 percent in the last five years. But that is only the median; in some parts of the country, prices have skyrocketed astronomically. In Los Angeles, the price of a single-family home rose more than 130 percent over that same five-year period. In Washington, prices went up 105 percent. Instead of traditional stocks and bonds, people are turning to real estate as the place to invest their hard-earned money.

Despite some economists' claim that the surge in real estate values cannot last, investing in real estate is one of the safer choices that a family can make. Unlike the volatile nature of stocks, which can fall apart as a group if the value of a large company drops suddenly, a home in good condition may retain its worth even if one nearby suffers a loss in value. An investor can also contribute directly toward increasing the value of their property. Once a property has been chosen, and at least part of the mortgage paid for, the value of the home, or equity, can then be applied to loans for making improvements to the property. Refurbishing, adding amenities like a pool or garage, or redecorating the interior can greatly increase the value of the home. Some buyers even choose to start over again. Often, even more profit can be turned by bulldozing the existing home to the ground, even if it's in good condition, and then building a new, larger home in its place.

Notes

Now have a friend read the following lecture on the same topic to you. Be sure to take notes as you listen.

📖 Reading, Summarizing Two Sources

Professor: So that's the history of the modern real estate boom in the United States. Many people are investing all of their savings into properties, and to be honest, some of them are making huge profits. But the question many economists are asking is, how long can this . . . ahh . . . boom last?

There are a couple of factors that need to be looked at. First, to get into the market as quickly as possible, many real estate investors are taking out higher-risk, higher-interest loans because they can be approved faster. The thinking is that the value of the home will go up faster than the interest on the loan, so in a few years, the buyer can sell the home for a profit. But, with prices going higher and higher, there is going to be a point at which the average home buyer won't be able to afford the average home.

Second, people forget that the astronomical growth that has occurred was based on home prices from the 1990s. Buying a home now won't result in the same amazing profit as it did five or ten years ago, because the current prices of homes are already inflated. The boom can't continue forever, and once the bottom falls out of the market, investors will be stuck with a nightmare: homes that are worth less than the loans they were bought with.

Notes

Now write a short summary that includes combined information from both the passage and the lecture telling what you have learned about regulation and deregulation. Try using some of the following expressions as you write:

- To show similarities: *similarly, likewise, also, as well, like, both*
- To show differences: *however, on the other hand, although, yet, whereas, unlike, in contrast*

_____
_____
_____
_____
_____
_____
_____
_____
_____
_____
_____
_____
_____
_____
_____
_____
_____
_____
_____
_____
_____

Answer: Responses will vary, but here is one sample summary.

Sample Response: The Real Estate Boom

The housing market in the United States is growing at an amazing rate. Some Americans are even investing in homes instead of the stock market, because real estate seems to be a more stable investment. The prices of single-family homes have gone up more than 100 percent in a several different parts of the country. However, not all economists agree that real estate is a good long-term investment. Some investors who are in a hurry to get into the market are taking on risky loans, counting on the value of the home to increase fast enough that they do not end up losing money on the property. While this strategy seems to be working in the present, some fear that the strong market will not last in the long term and that many investors will be stuck with debt they cannot afford to repay.

Compare and Contrast

There are two basic ways of writing a compare and contrast text. One is called the *point-by-point format,* and the other is called the *block format.* You will study these text types in detail in the writing chapter, but a quick way to recognize these two formats is to ask yourself the following questions about the body of the essay:

- Are the objects of comparison discussed in separate paragraphs?
- Does the body begin with a discussion of the features of one object and then move on, in later paragraphs, to a comparison with the features of a second object?

If so, the text is written in block format. If not, ask yourself the following questions:

- Are the two (or more) objects being compared discussed in the same paragraphs?
- Does the body begin with a discussion of how both objects compare in regards to one feature and then move on to compare the two objects on the basis of other features?

If so, the text is written in point-by-point format.

Now read the following text, "The Future of Air Travel."

The Future of Air Travel

With the growing price of fuel and consumer demand for lower-priced tickets, the airline industry is facing an important decision in the early part of the 21st century. Customers want to fly across the globe for business and leisure, but the question is: what is the most cost-effective way to get them to their destinations? For airline companies to make a profit, they need to balance the cost of operations, including salaries, fuel, maintenance, and airport fees, among other factors, against the amount of money they make by ferrying people from one point to another. This is referred to as the passenger yield, and the point at which an aircraft is paying for its own expenses is called the breakeven load. If an air carrier cannot keep profits well above the breakeven load, the entire company is at risk.

Aircraft manufacturers have invested heavily in trying to solve this problem by offering very different solutions. Two brand-new aircraft designs are on the market for airlines to choose from. The first is a European-built, 600-ton super jumbo jet that will seat between 550 and 800 passengers. The second is a much smaller, 240-ton jet built in the United States that will seat between 250 and 300 passengers.

The larger of the two aircraft is a first in many ways. The largest commercial aircraft ever built, it has a range of approximately 8,000 miles and a top speed of around 610 miles an hour. With a wingspan of over 260 feet, this aircraft is intended for long flights between major airports. Because of its enormous size, only a few airports in the world are currently capable of handling such a giant aircraft, and most airports will not only have to widen their runways, but they will also have to buy new gangways to handle the two levels of passengers that will be getting on and off the oversized plane. The smaller plane has a slightly higher top speed of around 650 miles an hour and a range of between 3,500 and 8,000 miles, depending on the model. With a wingspan of around 200 feet, it is small enough to land at most airports that can handle medium-sized jet traffic.

Both aircraft take advantage of the most recent advances in technology, like carbon fiber to reduce weight and increase strength and quieter, more efficient engines. Typically, aircraft are constructed of aluminum, used for its strength, light weight, and low cost. In recent times, the use of woven composite fibers has become popular, because the final material is much lighter and stronger and can be formed into complex shapes more easily than aluminum. However, composites have not been used for long, and some experts are unsure how composites will withstand the constant stresses that aircraft frames must endure. The larger aircraft uses composites in less than 25 percent of its construction, because composites cost up to 500 percent more than the standard aircraft aluminum, making a 79-foot-high, 239-foot-long fuselage prohibitively expensive. The smaller plane was designed with composite materials in more than 50 percent of its construction; the increased aerodynamics and lower weight make it one of the most efficient passenger aircraft currently flying.

Despite their similar ranges, these aircraft represent very different philosophies of air travel. The designers of the larger craft believe that airlines will be most profitable by transporting large numbers of people between major airports, or hubs, and then people will fly from the hubs to smaller airports closer to their final destinations. By flying bigger planes, the airline will be able to have fewer flights, which should push income well above the breakeven load. On the other hand, the smaller plane is designed to meet a very different anticipated need. Its designers predict that people will demand more direct flight service between smaller airports and that people prefer not to have to transfer from one plane to another at busy hubs. The smaller design means that it will be easier for airlines to fill each flight to capacity, maximizing passenger yield, and the lower operating cost and increased efficiency of the smaller plane mean that airlines will be able to afford more aircraft.

Whether the record-breaking jumbo jet or the small, composite-built airplane will dominate the skies of the future remains to be determined. Certainly, whichever design philosophy prevails, whether massive delivery to local hubs or increased numbers of smaller, point-to-point flights, the newest generation of passenger jets will shape the airline business of tomorrow.

First decide in which type of format "The Future of Air Travel" is written. Then make an outline of how you could reorganize the text in the other format. A space is provided below for your outline.

I.

_____

_____

II.

_____

_____

III.
_____

_____
IV.
_____

_____

The passage is written in point-by-point format. Here is a sample block format outline.

I. Intro: Need for new aircraft
II. Jumbo jet design
   A. Design philosophy
   B. Specifications and construction
   C. Performance
III. Smaller jet design
   A. Design philosophy
   B. Specifications and construction
   C. Performance
IV. Conclusion

Understanding the question types is critical for knowing how and where to apply your strategies. Keep reading to learn more.

PRACTICE: READING QUESTIONS

There are several question types on the Reading section of the TOEFL. We have already reviewed eight types in Chapters 1, 5, and 9:

1. Drawing an inference

2. Summarizing the most important points

3. Understanding rhetorical function

4. Understanding details

5. Understanding details as they relate to the main idea (schematic table)

6. Inferring word meaning from context

7. Locating a referent

8. Understanding coherence

In this chapter, we will continue to review drawing an inference questions, and we will introduce the final question type:

- Paraphrasing

Question Type 1 Review: Drawing an Inference

There are three to five passages in the Reading section of the TOEFL. Each passage is followed by zero to two inference questions.

One particularly difficult reading skill to master is the skill of drawing inferences. A good inference is one that is supported by information in the text but that is not directly stated. Look at the following sentences from the passage.

> With the growing price of fuel and consumer demand for lower-priced tickets, the airline industry is facing an important decision in the early part of the 21st century. Customers want to fly across the globe for business and leisure, but the question is: what is the most cost-effective way to get them to their destinations?

Based on these sentences we can infer that:

- Airlines do not have a very profitable solution to meet current costs and customer expectations. This is a good inference, because although the airlines' current operational models are not discussed in the passage, the fact that they "face an important decision" means that current business models are not meeting business needs.
- Customers will not accept higher ticket prices caused by higher fuel costs. This is also a good inference, because the first sentence tells us that there is consumer demand for lower-priced tickets.

In attempting to draw a good inference, it is important to pay attention to dates and numbers. Key words such as those in the following list can be equally useful when reading for what is implied.

- *Not only/not exclusively*
- *Many/most/much of*
- *Some/several/a few*
- *May/can/could*
- *Used to be/was/were*
- *At one time/previously*

As you answer the following questions, be aware of these key words and any others that will help you make good inferences.

To answer inference questions correctly, you will also need to avoid distracters. The types of distracters for this type of question include:

- Answer choices that include words from the passage but that are untrue.
- Answer choices that you think are true based on previous knowledge or intuition but are unsupported by information in the passage.

Based on the information in paragraph two, what can be inferred about passenger yield?

(A) It is more important than the cost of moving passengers.

(B) It determines whether an aircraft flight is cancelled.

(C) It is the ratio of cost of operation to income from ticket sales.

(D) It is calculated before passengers board the aircraft.

Answer: Choice (A) is not correct because it is untrue. The passage says that passenger yield is the ratio between cost and ticket sales. Choice (B) is not correct, because although it includes words from the passage, it is not supported by the passage. The passage does not say there is a cause-and-effect relationship between the passenger yield and the cancellation of flights. Choice (D) is incorrect, because the passage does not support this information, whether or not it is true. Choice (C) is correct, because the information is supported by the following statement:

> For airline companies to make a profit, they need to balance the cost of operations, including salaries, fuel, maintenance, and airport fees, among other factors, against the amount of money they make by ferrying people from one point to another. This is referred to as the passenger yield . . . .

Based on information in paragraph two, what can be inferred about aircraft manufacturers?

Ⓐ They assist airlines in determining ticket prices.

Ⓑ They rely heavily on government investment to develop new aircraft.

Ⓒ Without airlines, they have no customers to sell to.

Ⓓ They have an interest in anticipating the needs of the airline industry.

Answer: Choice (A) is incorrect because it is not supported in paragraph two, regardless of whether it is true or not. Choice (B) is incorrect. Paragraph two includes words similar to those in the answer choice, but it does not give any indication that this choice is true. Choice (C) is incorrect, because nothing in paragraph two supports this information. Choice (D) is correct, because it can be inferred that the aircraft manufacturers have an interest in anticipating the needs of the airline industry:

> Aircraft manufacturers have invested heavily in trying to solve this problem . . . .

> Based on information in paragraph three, what can be inferred about the larger airplane?
>
> (A) It is only designed for long flights between major airports.
>
> (B) At this time, it cannot land at most airports.
>
> (C) It is not intended to carry only cargo.
>
> (D) Runways will have to be lengthened for it to land.

Answer: Choice (A) is not correct, because although it includes words from the passage, the answer is incorrect. Choice (B) is correct, because one can infer that the larger airplane cannot land at most airports from the statement:

> Because of its enormous size, only a few airports in the world are currently capable of handling such an enormous aircraft, and most airports will not only have to widen their runways . . . .

Choice (C) is incorrect, because the paragraph does not imply that the aircraft is not intended to carry only cargo. Choice (D) is incorrect because this answer is not supported by the paragraph.

> According to paragraph five, what can be inferred about airline hubs?
>
> (A) Smaller jets do not fly to hubs.
>
> (B) They handle more traffic than smaller airports.
>
> (C) More important hubs are located close to major cities.
>
> (D) There are fewer hubs than smaller airports.

Answer: Choice (D) is the correct answer, because the reader can infer that there are fewer hubs than smaller airports.

Now look at the following sentences and sets of sentences from the text. What can you infer from each?

1. Typically aircraft are constructed of aluminum, used for its strength, light weight, and low cost. In recent times, the use of woven composite fibers has become popular, because the final material is much lighter and stronger and can be formed into complex shapes more easily than aluminum.

   _____

   _____

2. The smaller plane was designed with composite materials in more than 50 percent of its construction; the increased aerodynamics and lower weight make it one of the most efficient passenger aircraft currently flying.

   _____

   _____

3. The designers of the larger craft believe that airlines will be most profitable by transporting large numbers of people between major airports, or hubs, and then people will fly from the hubs to smaller airports closer to their final destinations.

   _____

   _____

4. On the other hand, the smaller plane is designed to meet a very different anticipated need. Its designers predict that people will demand more direct flight service between smaller airports and that people prefer not to have to transfer from one plane to another at busy hubs.

   _____

   _____

Answers:

1. Newer aircraft are more likely to have composite components than older aircraft.

2. Use of composite materials can make an airplane more efficient.

3. The designers believe that short flights from hubs to smaller airports are not as profitable as long flights between hubs.

4. Passenger preference was a factor in the design of the smaller aircraft.

Question Type 9: Paraphrasing

There are three to five passages in the Reading section of the TOEFL. Each passage is followed by zero or one paraphrasing question.

Throughout this book you will notice that you are often asked to rewrite sentences or paragraphs in your own words. Rewriting sentences using your own words, also called paraphrasing, is extremely important both in university work and for the TOEFL. Paraphrasing questions ask you to choose the answer that best expresses the meaning of a sentence in a reading passage. Incorrect answers either:

- change the meaning of the sentence
  OR
- do not include all of the information in the sentence.

Which of the sentences below is the best paraphrase of the following sentence?

However, composites have not been used for long, and some experts are unsure how composites will withstand the constant stresses that aircraft frames must endure.

(A) Composites fail under high stress conditions.

(B) Experts believe that composites are not safe construction materials.

(C) The reliability of composite materials has not yet been established.

(D) Composites have not been well tested and will not stand up to rigorous abuse.

Answer: Choice (A) is incorrect, because it changes the meaning of the original sentence, which does not state that composites will fail under high stress conditions. Choice (B) is incorrect, because it is too vague and does not include all of the information in the original sentence. It states that composites are not safe, while the passage specifically refers to the construction of aircraft frames. Choice (C) is the best choice, because it uses synonyms effectively and has a change in word order without changing the meaning of the sentence. Choice (D) is incorrect because nothing in the original sentence implies that composites will not stand up to stress, only that they have not been fully tested yet.

Which of the sentences below is the best paraphrase of the following sentence?

The smaller design means that it will be easier for airlines to fill each flight to capacity, maximizing passenger yield, and the lower operating cost and increased efficiency of the smaller plane mean that airlines will be able to afford more aircraft.

(A) Airlines will be able to afford to purchase more, smaller aircraft due to operational savings and improved passenger yield.

(B) Investing in smaller aircraft will ensure that most flights will be filled to capacity.

(C) Lower operating costs mean that airlines will be able to afford to purchase more small aircraft.

(D) Smaller aircraft have a better maximum yield than large aircraft and are therefore more efficient.

Answer: Choice (A) is the correct answer. It uses synonyms effectively and has a change in word order without changing the meaning of the sentence. The sentence from the passage does not suggest that investing in smaller aircraft "ensures" that flights will be filled to capacity, so (B) is incorrect. Choice (C) omits the important point that lower operating costs combined with better passenger yield and increased efficiency can make it possible to buy more aircraft. Choice (D) is incorrect because it suggests that smaller aircraft have a better maximum yield than large aircraft, something not suggested in the original sentence.

As you can see, paraphrasing effectively requires the use of synonyms and the ability to change word form and structure. Practice these techniques by paraphrasing the following sentences.

1. If an air carrier cannot keep profits well above the breakeven load, the entire company is at risk.

   _____

   _____

2. Aircraft manufacturers have invested heavily in trying to solve this problem by offering very different solutions.

   _____

   _____

3. Both aircraft take advantage of the most recent advances in technology, like carbon fiber to reduce weight and increase strength, and quieter, more efficient engines.

   _____

   _____

4. The designers of the larger craft believe that airlines will be most profitable by transporting large numbers of people between major airports, or hubs, and then people will fly from the hubs to smaller airports closer to their final destinations.

   _____

   _____

Answers: Answers will vary, but here are some sample paraphrased sentences:

1. To make a profit, airlines must take in more money than it takes to operate their planes and equipment.

2. Several different designs have been created to increase airline passenger yield.

3. Both aircraft make use of lower-weight materials and improved engines.

4. The big craft is designed to move large numbers of people between large, busy airports; then the passengers will use local transportation to get where they want to go.

When you are ready, move on to the Writing chapter.

Chapter 14:
Writing: Compare and Contrast

This chapter covers two types of essays found on the TOEFL. These are:

1. Compare/contrast essays

2. Essays in response to a reading passage and a lecture

Recognizing Compare/Contrast Essay Prompts

There are two tasks in the Writing section of the TOEFL. The second is a 30-minute essay based on a single prompt. In the Writing section's second task, you must write an essay based only on a short prompt that asks you to describe or explain something or to express an opinion on an issue. You do not need any specialized knowledge to write this essay. The prompt is based on topics that will be familiar to all test takers. You are given 30 minutes to plan, write, and revise this essay. Typically, an effective essay will include a minimum of 300 words. Essays will be judged on the quality of the writing, including idea development, organization, and the quality and accuracy of the language used to express the ideas.

One of the essay types that you may need to write for this second Writing section task is the compare/contrast essay. In a compare/contrast essay, you will discuss the ways in which two topics are similar (comparing them), and the ways in which they differ (contrasting them). Sometimes this analysis will be the only requirement of the prompt. Most times, however, the prompt will ask you to identify your own preference among the options and to use comparison and contrast to support your point of view.

How will you recognize a prompt that requires a compare/contrast essay in response? There are several ways. Let's consider two of them:

1. The prompt will usually suggest two or more related topics and ask you to make observations about the features of all of them.

> Which do you think is more important, investing in recycling programs or researching for more environmentally friendly materials? Explain your preference by describing the advantages and disadvantages of each.

2. The prompt may ask you to decide between two options and explain your reasons for doing so. Comparative or superlative (-er or -est) forms of adjectives and adverbs in the prompt will indicate that a compare/contrast essay would be appropriate.

> Some people feel that the most important focus of education should be addressing the individual needs of students. Others feel that education should be centered on a core curriculum that all students must learn. In your view, which of these educational philosophies is stronger? Use specific examples and reasons in your answer.

Read the following prompts and circle those that require a compare/contrast essay in response. Then write what kind of essay is required for the others.

1. Some people suggest that children should be allowed to leave school for work at age 16. Do you agree with this view? Why or why not?

2. Many people like to structure their free time. Others prefer to leave their free time unplanned. Which kind of person are you? Provide reasons and examples to support your answer.

3. Many people travel by either public or private transportation. Which do you prefer to use? Explain your preference by describing the differences and similarities between the two.

Answers:

1. This prompt requires an agree/disagree essay.

2. This prompt requires a descriptive essay.

3. This prompt requires a compare/contrast essay.

Creating a Thesis Statement for a Compare/Contrast Essay

Usually, a compare/contrast essay prompt will require you to choose between the options or points of view it mentions. You will express that choice in your essay's introduction as a thesis statement, a clear statement of your opinion or point of view, then devote the rest of your essay to supporting it.

Writing Topic Sentences

Once you have a thesis statement, your next task is to create topic sentences to introduce each of your body paragraphs. Your topic sentences should identify the general topic you intend to address in each of your body paragraphs.

Let's use the following sample response to a prompt requiring you to compare and contrast the advantages of working for a large or small company.

Compare/Contrast Essay: Sample Response

Would you prefer to work for a large company or a small company? Explain why.

Preference: large company

Small company advantages:

- Friendlier
- Easier to make an impression
- Greater autonomy

Large company advantages:

- Greater resources
- Higher salary
- Opportunities for posting in foreign countries
- Better on resume

Because each topic—small companies and large companies—has a different set of points to discuss, the sample uses a block format essay. Therefore, the first body paragraph will be about the advantages of smaller companies. The second body paragraph will be a discussion of the superior advantages of larger companies. So the following topic sentences are used to introduce each body paragraph:

- Small companies do offer certain advantages.
- Although small companies offer some advantages, they are outweighed by the advantages of working for a large, multinational company.

Both of these sentences are general enough to include all the points needed in each of the body paragraphs. The second topic sentence has the added feature of reminding the reader of the writer's point of view: that larger companies are superior to smaller companies as places of employment. Notice also that the second topic sentence begins with the word *although,* a transition signal telling the reader that the following discussion will contrast with what went before.

Structuring a Compare/Contrast Essay

Compare/contrast essays can be written in one of two different patterns of organization. As an example, let's compare and contrast apples and oranges. Look at the two outlines that follow, both for the body of an essay that compares and contrasts apples and oranges.

Outline A: Block Format	Outline B: Point-by-Point Format
Paragraph 1: Apples a. Color b. Flavor c. Varieties Paragraph 2: Oranges a. Color b. Flavor c. Varieties	Paragraph 1: Color of apples and oranges Paragraph 2: Flavor of apples and orange Paragraph 3: Varieties of apples and oranges

Consider the differences in the organization of the two essays that would be written from these two outlines. Answer the following questions.

1. Which outline deals with apples in one paragraph and oranges in another?

   _____

2. Which outline discusses apples and oranges within the same paragraph?

   _____

3. What features of apples and oranges are mentioned in both outlines?

   _____

4. Which outline mentions all of the features in the same paragraph?

_____

5. Which outline mentions one feature per paragraph?

_____

Answers:

1. (A) Block format

2. (B) Point-by-point format

3. Colors, flavors, and varieties

4. (A) Block format

5. (B) Point-by-point format

Block Format

In block organization, each of the two items being compared and contrasted occupies a separate section of the essay. For example, the writer of the model essay, "The Future of Air Travel" in Chapter 13 on reading, might have chosen to present all the information about the large plane design in the first part of the essay and all the information about the smaller design in the second part of the essay. In this block format, each paragraph in the first section would have contained only information about the large design. There would be a paragraph in which the writer presented all the information about the plane's design specifications, another about the airplane's performance, and a third about features of the theory behind the plane. In the second half of the essay, there would have been another set of paragraphs on the same topics, but containing information about the smaller airplane instead of the larger.

Block format works best if you have more information about one of your topics than the other.

An outline of the block organization might look like this:

Block Format Outline

I. Introduction
II. Topic one
    A. Point one
    B. Point two
    C. Point three
    D. (Possible additional points)
III. Topic two
    A. Point one
    B. Point two
    C. Point three
    D. (Possible additional points)
IV. Conclusion

Point-by-Point Format

In this method of organization, each point of comparison or contrast occupies its own paragraph; within each paragraph, the author provides information about both topics as they relate to that point. For this reason, the point-by-point format works best if you have the same amount of information about each of your topics.

Here's an example outline for such an essay.

Point-by-Point Format Outline

I. Introduction
II. Point one
    A. Topic one
    B. Topic two
III. Point two
    A. Topic one
    B. Topic two
IV. Point three
    A. Topic one
    B. Topic two
V. Conclusion

Writing the Conclusion of a Compare/Contrast Essay

Often, conclusions are the most neglected part of an essay, partly because they come last and partly because writers are sometimes unsure of exactly what to do when the time comes to write a conclusion. In this chapter, you will learn strategies for solving both of those problems.

Budgeting Your Time

In timed writing conditions, when you have to plan, write, and proofread an essay within a given time limit, it is important to leave time to write a good conclusion. With practice, you will learn what system works best for you, but a good rule is that for a 30-minute essay, about 3–4 minutes are needed for each paragraph of your essay, including the conclusion. Here are some tips for writing an essay within a 30-minute time limit.

- Eight to ten minutes for prewriting and planning
- Fifteen minutes for writing (four to five paragraphs)
- Five minutes for editing and proofreading

Once you have practiced budgeting your time carefully, all sections of your essay will improve, and you will be able to feel more comfortable and relaxed as you write.

What Is the Function of a Conclusion?

The English word *conclude* has two meanings. The first meaning is simply to *come to an end*. For example, we might say:

- The meeting concluded on time.
- The movie concluded with an explosive scene.

On the other hand, *conclude* may mean to come to a decision after considering the available evidence. For instance, a person might say:

- I have concluded that X is the best course of action.
- After long deliberation, the jury concluded that the defendant was guilty as charged.

It is this second meaning of *conclude* that you should be thinking of when it is time to write the conclusion to your essay. A concluding paragraph is not simply the place where your essay comes to an end. Instead, it is the part of the essay that identifies the solution, resolution, or decision that is the logical outcome of the discussion and information you have provided in the essay body.

Here are two rules to keep in mind as you write your conclusion.

1. **The job of your conclusion is to identify or emphasize the lesson, message, or decision to which the essay discussion logically leads the reader.** This lesson or message should agree with or confirm the thesis presented in the introduction. A brief summary of your main points from the body may help to lead your reader to that message.

2. **Long conclusions are unnecessary.** It is best to avoid introducing any new information or arguments in the conclusion—those belong in the body of the essay.

Read the conclusion of the essay on aircraft again:

> Whether the record-breaking jumbo jet or the small, composite-built airplane will dominate the skies of the future remains to be determined. Certainly, whichever design philosophy prevails, whether it is massive delivery to local hubs or increased numbers of smaller, point-to-point flights, the newest generation of passenger jets will shape the airline business of tomorrow.

Now answer the following questions.

1. How well does this conclusion demonstrate the two rules previously given? Is it long-winded?

   _____

   _____

2. Does it introduce new information?

_____

_____

_____

3. Does it present a solution or resolution that follows from the essay's discussion?

_____

_____

_____

4. Which of the two meanings of *conclude* is demonstrated by this concluding paragraph?

_____

_____

_____

Answers:

1. It partially answers the question asked in the beginning of the passage: How can airlines move passengers cheaply?

2. No.

3. Partially—it restates that aircraft design will be a major factor in how airlines modernize.

4. It identifies part of the solution to the question asked in the beginning of the passage.

Now try to apply the strategies for budgeting time and for writing conclusions discussed in this chapter by completing the following Compare/Contrast Essay Practice.

PRACTICE: ESSAY WRITING

Try to apply the strategies for budgeting time and for writing conclusions discussed in the chapter.

> Write an essay in which you describe the similarities and differences between the business culture of your own country and that of another country.

_____

_____

_____

_____

_____

_____

_____

_____

_____

_____

_____

_____

_____

_____

_____

_____

_____

_____

_____

_____

_____

_____

_____

_____

_____

_____

_____

_____

_____

_____

_____

_____

_____

_____

_____

_____

_____

_____

_____

_____

_____

_____

_____

_____

_____

_____

_____

_____

Answer: Essays will vary, but here is a sample.

Sample Compare/Contrast Essay: Business Cultures

The United States and Japan are very different countries culturally speaking, and the way business is conducted in each can be very confusing to visitors. Even social actions that one might think of as simple, such as greeting a new person, attending a meeting, or socializing after work, can be very different.

For example, when two people meet for the first time in a business setting in the United States, it is customary to shake hands, say, "Nice to meet you," and perhaps ask a very simple question like, "How are you?" In Japan, the custom is very different. When two people meet for the first time, it is expected that both will bow to a specific depth, depending on the status of the other person, and both will exchange business cards by holding them out with two hands. When someone gives out a business card, the receiver must then carefully put the card away in a pocket so as to show a proper level of respect to its owner.

Business meetings are very different, too. In the United States, when an important business meeting is held, it may be to gather the appropriate people together in a room to make a decision. In this case, everyone who is invited to the meeting is expected to participate, and more often than not, any person in the meeting may speak if they have a valuable and relevant contribution to the conversation. In Japan, a business meeting is more likely to be called when higher levels of management need to inform their staff of a decision that has been made. In these meetings, only senior members of the staff participate in any discussion that takes place.

Last comes social activity after work. While in the United States, it is not uncommon for groups of people to occasionally go out after work, socializing is for the most part a voluntary activity. On the other hand, in Japanese business culture, it is expected that employees will go out quite often after work with their coworkers and perhaps even their superiors. This is sometimes seen as an important teambuilding exercise, and the highest-ranking person in a group will often end up paying the largest portion of the bill as a courtesy to the rest of the employees.

Despite all of these differences, business relations between Japan and the United States seem to be going strong. Every day people are flying across the Pacific Ocean in both directions. With a little studying and an open mind, they will be prepared to do business in a different culture.

Now you will have an opportunity to practice taking notes, summarizing, paraphrasing, and writing a response to a prompt. Following is an example of the first task in the Writing section of the TOEFL.

Writing an Essay in Response to a Reading Passage and a Lecture

There are two tasks in the Writing section of the TOEFL. The first is a 20-minute essay based on a reading passage and a lecture.

For the first essay in the TOEFL Writing section, you will have three minutes to read a passage about an academic topic. You may take notes as you read. Then you will listen to a lecture about the same topic and take notes while you listen. Information in the lecture will conflict somewhat with the information in the reading passage; that is, a different perspective on the topic will be presented.

After reading and listening, you will have 20 minutes to write a response to a question that asks you about the relationship between the reading and the lecture. The question will not ask you to express your opinion. You will be able to see the reading passage again when it is time for you to write, and you will be able to use the notes you took while reading and listening.

An effective response will be approximately 150–225 words long. It will be judged on the quality of your writing and on its completeness and accuracy.

> You will have three minutes to read the following passage. You may take notes. After reading the passage, you will hear a short lecture on a related topic. Again, you may take notes while you listen.

Language Learning

There are different theories that attempt to explain how people learn a second language, two of which are the "nativist" theory and the "environmentalist" theory. The nativist theory proposes that the process of learning a second language is the same as the process of learning a first language. According to nativism, humans have an innate biological function that allows them to process and acquire language, regardless of whether it is a first language learned as an infant or a second language learned later in life.

In 1965, Noam Chomsky proposed that all children utilize an innate process, or an internal "language acquisition device," to learn their first language. Chomsky hypothesized that when humans are born, they are born with basic knowledge of the rules and structures of a language. Chomsky believed that humans learn the complex rules of their mother tongue at a very rapid pace and that this pace cannot be attributed to external language input. Therefore, it must be due to a biological function.

In 1967, Eric Lenneberg also proposed that language acquisition is an innate process that allows humans to learn a language best between the age of two and puberty. This theory, called the "critical period hypothesis," suggests that upon reaching puberty, the two hemispheres of the brain begin functioning independently, causing a neurological change that makes learning new languages nearly impossible.

In essence, Chomsky and Lenneberg believed that humans have a special ability to acquire languages in their early years and that, if this ability is not exercised during this period, they lose the ability to learn and process language.

Notes

🔊 Lecture: Language Learning

Narrator: Listen to part of a talk on the topic you just read about.

Professor (male): We talked earlier about the nativist view of language acquisition shared by Lenneberg and Chomsky . . . that language learners use an innate "language acquisition device" to help them learn a language. Nativists theorize that the critical period for learning a language is somewhere between age 2 and 13 or 14, at which point our brains change, making it nearly impossible to ever again achieve native-like proficiency in a second language.

But how many of you know of people who've learned a second language as adults and can speak it really well? And how do the nativists' theories explain a student who begins learning a foreign language at age ten but never really becomes proficient? Shouldn't their internal "language acquisition device" kick in . . . since their brains haven't changed yet? Nativists suggest that biological factors rule language learning, but there are other schools of thought as well.

Some modern linguists—called "environmental-ists"—believe that the environment in which a student is taught determines how well that student learns a language. John Schumann argues that students who don't have the opportunity . . . or the desire . . . to practice speaking the language won't learn the language . . . regardless of age or ability. He says it's especially beneficial if language learn-ers can practice speaking with native speakers . . . perhaps even integrate into a community where the language is spoken.

Environmentalists believe that the crucial element of language learning is the interaction that learners have with the language, whether this interaction takes place with other speakers of the language or with input from other

sources like television or radio. But what's crucial . . . is that
the more often learners hear and speak the language, the
more successful they'll be in understanding the language.

You have 20 minutes to plan and write your response. Your response
will be judged on the basis of the quality of your writing and on how
well your response presents the points in the lecture and their relationship to the reading passage. Typically, an effective response will
be 150 to 225 words.

> What are the similarities between the the points of view
> expressed in the reading passage and the short talk? What
> are the differences? Which position is stronger? Use details
> and examples to support your answer.

_____

_____

_____

_____

_____

_____

_____

_____

_____

_____

_____

_____

_____

_____

_____

_____

_____

_____

Sample Essay

Responses will vary. Here is a sample essay.

Sample Response to a Reading Passage and a Lecture: Learning Language

The study of how people learn language has divided into two schools of thought. The author of the passage points out that children who are learning language quickly start using the rules and structures of a language, even if they are too young to understand that they are doing so. The writer claims that this must be due to some biological mechanism that allows us to learn language so quickly.

The speaker doesn't disagree that language learning might be partly biological but says that the environment in which a student is learning is an important factor in whether the student retains the language. What that means is that, if the student doesn't have some sort of personal reason or motivation for learning and opportunities to practice the language, the student will find it very hard to learn.

Both the speaker and the writer make good points. But I think that the speaker makes a stronger argument when mentioning that not all children who study a language while they are young learn to speak it well. It seems to me that learning a language depends mostly on the social reasons a child might have for studying, and certainly on the opportunities that the child has to practice using it.

Now that you have practiced both types of TOEFL Writing section essays, you are ready to begin the next chapter.

Chapter 15:
Listening: Inference

Note-Taking

Remember that as you listen to the passages on the TOEFL, you should be taking notes. You must:

- Listen for strong statements by the speaker that indicate the speaker's opinion and attitude
- Write down key words, names, numbers, dates, or anything else you think is important

Listen to a conversation between a peer advisor and a student. Take notes as you listen. The audio is transcribed below. Have a friend read the transcript to you and take notes on what you hear.

🔊 Listening, Note-Taking

Narrator: Listen to a dialogue between a student and a peer advisor.

Student: I'm not sure if I'm in the right office. Is this the peer advisement?

Peer advisor: It is. Hi, I'm Matt. I'm one of the peer advisors.

Student: Oh? I didn't see a sign on the door.

Peer advisor: We're getting a new one. I was just about to stick up a temporary one when you walked in. So, how can I help you?

Student: Uh, [fumbling for paper] I saw this flier . . . here it is . . . I think I might be interested in the peer advisement program, but I don't know what it is exactly.

Peer Advisor: Well, I can explain. By the way, do you know we have an open house in about three weeks? We started putting up fliers about it.

Student: Mmm, I only found this general one.

Peer advisor: Okay. Well, in a nutshell, peer advisement is a great program—for psych majors especially—but anyone can participate because this program trains you. It has course work to supplement what you get in another major. So what are you majoring in?

Student: Psych, as a matter of fact.

Peer advisor: Great. You'll be able to, to overlap some of your classes then with ours. We've got some general courses on counseling methods and a series of seminars, and you'll have an internship for a year.

Student: Where would that be?

Peer advisor: Everything's done directly on campus. So you'd work right in this office, or maybe in another student-centered office like admissions or the bursar.

Student: Doing what?

Peer advisor: Mainly answering students' questions about the college . . . helping them feel comfortable here . . . making it easy to understand the requirements. The majority of students who come here are transfers, especially from overseas. Many don't know exactly what to expect from an American college.

Student: Sounds like a valuable service.

Peer advisor: It sure is. I actually finished up my program already, but I'm volunteering to help out, and I even run one of the seminars now.

Student: Is there any, uh, like heavy-duty counseling? Like students who might have more, say, major problems?

Peer advisor: Well, sometimes. You can't avoid that, of course. But if a student needs more in-depth help, we can certainly refer them to someone who can help them. We have access to lots of resources both on and off campus.

Student: And when did you say the open house was?

Peer advisor: In about three weeks. Come! If you give me your e-mail address, I can send you a reminder.

Notes

Use your notes to answer the following questions.

1. What is the advisor's initial attitude toward the student?

_____

_____

2. What can you infer about the student?

_____

_____

3. Why didn't the student know about the open house?

_____

_____

4. Why does the advisor want to know the student's major?

_____

_____

5. What information does the advisor ask the student to provide?

_____

_____

Answers:

1. The advisor is helpful.
2. The student thinks counseling other students is worthwhile.
3. She had only seen a general flier about the program, not for the open house.
4. Because the student is a psych major, she can take some of the counseling courses for credit.
5. He asks for her email address.

Outlining

You know by now that an outline is a skeletal structure of a text. It contains the main and supporting ideas in the order they are presented but does not necessarily include any specific details.

The outlining of a conversation is different from the outlining of a lecture, because it involves constant turn taking between two people who have different viewpoints on the topic. One speaker can disagree with the other and introduce a new argument or even change the subject entirely. As a result, the natural speech of a conversation doesn't have the same carefully planned transitions found in lectures for moving from one supporting point to another.

For a conversation, you should try to identify the following elements:

- The two characters involved in the conversation
- The central character (the one who has a particular need)
- The central character's need
- The central character's conflict (who or what is preventing them from satisfying the need)
- The resolution of the conflict (how the need is satisfied)

Understanding the question types is critical for knowing how and where to apply your strategies. Keep reading to learn more.

PRACTICE: LISTENING QUESTIONS

There are several different question types on the Listening section of the TOEFL. The previous chapters covered the following types:

- Understanding rhetorical function
- Drawing an inference
- Understanding a speaker's implication
- Identifying the main idea
- Summarizing the most important ideas
- Understanding details

This chapter will review two question types, focusing on how they apply to conversations:

1. Drawing an inference

2. Understanding a speaker's implication

Question Type 1 Review: Drawing an Inference

There are two or three conversations and four to six lectures in the Listening section of the TOEFL.

Remember that inference questions ask you to draw conclusions about specific details in what you hear or to make comparisons between details. To answer these types of questions, you should do the following:

- Listen carefully to the details of the lecture or conversation
- Try to understand unfamiliar words from context
- Listen for conditionals, intonation, and suggestions made by the speakers while the conversation is happening so that you can anticipate certain inference questions
- Use your knowledge about the situation to guess what sort of conclusion might be logical

The following are examples of inference questions:

- What probably happened to _____ ?
- What will _____ probably do next?
- What can be inferred about _____ ?

Now listen to a conversation between a manager in a bookstore and a student. Take notes as you listen. The conversation is transcribed below. Have a friend read the conversation to you.

🔊 Conversation: Bookstore Employment

Narrator: Listen to a dialogue between a student and a bookstore manager.

Student (male): May I please speak to, uh, someone in charge of the bookstore?

Manager (female): That's me. I'm Regina Watson, the manager. What can I do for you?

Student: I'm a freshman, and I'm, I'm looking for work at the college. I was wondering if maybe there's any part-time work available?

Manager: Well, [thinking] uh, yes, there is, there's a part-time position open at the moment.

Student: What kind of position is it?

Manager: Mostly cash register work. You've had experience working at a register?

Student: Yeah, this summer I've been working full-time as a cashier at the Five Star Diner downtown.

Manager: Oh, you did? Why, hmm, I thought you looked familiar. I eat there all the time.

Student: Well, now that you mention it, I do remember that you used to come in around five . . .

Manager: Yeah, five, five-thirty. Usually I'd stop by for dinner after work. So, you know what it's like to be working the register at a busy time then . . .

Student: Yeah, that I do. Dinner hour gets pretty crowded.

Manager: I'll say. Well, then you can imagine that next week, what with classes starting, this place'll be a madhouse.

Student: But you only have three registers. How do you manage?

Manager: For about a week and a half, we set up twice as many registers to handle the crowd. Plus we have a returns desk with two registers.

Student: Returns? So soon in the semester?

Manager: Oh yes, sometimes students pick up the wrong book by accident, or they decide to drop the course after a couple of classes.

Student: When things die down, what else would the, uh, job involve?

Manager: Well, we always need somebody at the register, of course, but then there are other responsibilities like inventory, and book orders for the next semester, and sweeping up. Everybody at the register rotates and pitches in.

Student: I wouldn't mind any of that.

Manager: Well, I'd be happy to consider you. No question we need to hire somebody soon. Could you stop by with a résumé later on today?

Student: I'm on my way home now and then headed off to work. It's my last week at the diner because my classes're starting next week. Say, maybe I could bring a copy of my résumé to the diner if you're going to stop by?

Manager: Actually, tonight I have to work late to check the stock. Tomorrow'd be just fine. Why don't you stop by here in the morning?

Student: Sounds good!

Notes

Following are several *inference* questions based on the conversation you heard between the professor and student about employment at the bookstore. Use your notes to answer the questions.

With which of the following statements would the manager probably agree?

Ⓐ Prior work experience is important for a new employee.

Ⓑ The student needs to get more experience.

Ⓒ Working in a restaurant is very different than working in a bookstore.

Ⓓ Working at a cash register is a madhouse.

Answer: This question tests your ability to make an inference based on several pieces of information within the entire lecture. Choices (B) and (C) twist facts from the conversation into the wrong context. The manager acknowledges the student's qualification for the job when asking, "So you know what it's like when . . . ." Choice (D) also misrepresents concepts from the lecture; they are discussing how working during a busy time can feel crazy. Choice (A) is the correct answer. When the manager finds out that the student is looking for a job, the manager's first question is whether the student has any prior experience.

The next inference question contains an excerpt from the conversation. Remember that on the actual test, you will only hear the excerpt—you will not be able to read it. Remember also that the question and the four answer choices in listening questions appear on the computer screen, but only the question is spoken by the narrator.

Narrator: Listen again to part of the conversation. Then answer the question.

Student: Returns? So soon in the semester?

What can be inferred by the student's statement?

(A) The student is frustrated that students waste money buying unnecessary books.

(B) The student is surprised that students return books right after starting class.

(C) The student believes the manager must be mistaken about the timing.

(D) The student thinks the store should not accept returned goods until later in the semester.

Answer: This question tests your ability to make an inference based on a single statement. Choice (A) is incorrect, because the student does not mention money or unnecessary books in the sentence. Choices (C) and (D) are inferences that are too extreme, especially considering that the student is trying to get a job from the store manager. Choice (B) is correct.

What will the student probably do tomorrow morning?

(A) Bring a copy of their résumé to the diner.

(B) Work as a cashier at the bookstore.

(C) Quit their job at the diner.

(D) Bring a copy of their resume to the manager.

Answer: Answering this question successfully requires an understanding of the entire lecture. Choice (A) is tempting, because the student uses these words the last time she speaks, but (A) is incorrect—the manager will not be at the diner. Choices (B) and (C) are also incorrect, because there is not enough information to predict whether the student will do either of these things. The manager asks the student to bring a copy to the bookstore the following morning, and the student's response is positive, so (D) is correct.

Narrator: Listen again to part of the conversation. Then answer the question.

Student: Yeah, that I do. Dinner hour gets pretty crowded.

What can be inferred about the speaker?

Ⓐ He thinks that the restaurant is crowded for an hour.

Ⓑ He understands what it is like to work in a busy place.

Ⓒ He thinks that dinner should last an hour.

Ⓓ He agrees that he can work at crowded diners.

Answer: Choice (A) is incorrect, because it uses words from the sentence but not in the correct context. There are no clues in the conversation to suggest that choice (C) or (D) is correct. Therefore, choice (B) is the correct answer.

What can be inferred about business at the bookstore?

Ⓐ The bookstore expects to become a very successful business.

Ⓑ It is busy at the beginning of the semester but slows down after a few weeks.

Ⓒ The number of book returns is severely affecting the bookstore's profits.

Ⓓ The business is very slow but constant.

Answer: Choice (A) is incorrect, because the manager never describes the success of the bookstore. Choice (C) is incorrect, because this inference is too broad, and it requires information that the manager did not provide in the conversation. Choice (D) is incorrect, because if business was consistently slow, they wouldn't have discussed working during a busy period. Choice (B) is a correct inference, because the manager talks about having to change the number of registers in the store during the first few weeks of school.

Question Type 2 Review: Understanding a Speaker's Implication

There are two or three conversations and four to six lectures in the Listening section of the TOEFL.

Remember from your review of this question type in Chapter 7 on listening that something that is implied is not directly stated. An implication is the meaning of a statement that is not obvious in the literal meaning of the words.

The answer choices for implication questions will contain situations that will further challenge you, because they were not discussed or did not occur. You will also see synonyms, homophones (words with different spellings but the same pronunciation; for example: *our* and *hour*), or other words repeated in the answer choices that are either out of context or not stated in the conversation.

The following are examples of implication questions:

- What does the man probably mean?
- What does the man suggest/imply?
- What does the woman want to know?
- Why does _____ say _____ ?
- What does _____ mean by _____ ?

Following are some sample speaker's implication questions. Each question includes an excerpt from the conversation between the student and manager about an on-campus job. First, listen to the question, and then look at the transcript and answer the question. Remember that on the test, you will hear everything printed here, but you will not see the transcript of the excerpt from the conversation.

Narrator: Listen again to part of the conversation. Then answer the question.

Manager: Well, we always need somebody at the register, of course, but then there are other responsibilities like inventory, and book orders for the next semester, and sweeping up. Everybody at the register rotates and pitches in.

What does the manager mean by saying this: "Everybody at the register rotates and pitches in."

(A) The cashiers have to move around a lot while they are at the register.

(B) All employees are expected to work at one register.

(C) The cashiers will have to work at other positions in the bookstore.

(D) The student will be expected to play on the bookstore softball team.

Answer: Choice (A) is incorrect. This distracter is focused on the verbs *rotate*, meaning "to move from one position to another," and *pitch in*, meaning "to help." If you do not know the meaning of these words, you may still recognize them as verbs and find answer (A) attractive. Choice (D) is also playing with the meanings of *rotate* and *pitch in*. Choice (B) is incorrect, because the manager is not saying that all employees are expected to use a particular register but that they are expected to do more jobs than just work at the cash register. Therefore, choice (C) is correct.

Narrator: Listen again to part of the conversation. Then answer the question.

Manager: I'll say. Well, then you can imagine that next week, what with classes starting, this place'll be a madhouse.

What does the manager probably mean?

(A) Students are crazy at the beginning of the semester.

(B) The bookstore will be a mess next week.

(C) The bookstore will not be able to handle the increase in business.

(D) The bookstore will be extremely busy at the beginning of the semester.

Answer: Choice (A) takes the term *madhouse* literally, mistakenly saying that students will be crazy rather than that the bookstore will be a "crazy" place to work. Choices (B) and (C) are similar ideas that incorrectly play with the meaning of *madhouse*. Choice (D) best represents what the manager means.

Narrator: Listen again to part of the conversation. Then answer the question.

Manager: Yeah, five, five-thirty. Usually I'd stop by for dinner after work. So, you know what it's like to be working the register at a busy time then . . .

What can be inferred from the manager's statement?

Ⓐ The manager thinks that the student's work is often busy.

Ⓑ The diner is not usually very busy.

Ⓒ The manager has been in the diner when it was busy.

Ⓓ The manager wants to know what working at a register is like.

Answer: Choices (A) and (B) are incorrect even though they use information from the conversation. Nothing in the conversation indicates whether the diner is "often busy" or "not usually busy." Answer (D) is incorrect, because the manager is not asking the student a question. Answer (C) is the best choice.

Narrator: Listen again to part of the conversation. Then answer the question.

Manager: For about a week and a half, we set up twice as many registers to handle the crowd. Plus we have a returns desk with two registers.

Student: Returns? So soon in the semester?

Manager: Oh yes, sometimes students pick up the wrong book by accident, or they decide to drop the course after a couple of classes.

Student: When things die down, what else would the, uh, job involve?

What does the student want to know when saying: "When things die down, what else would the, uh, job involve?"

(A) What the cashiers will do after the store goes out of business

(B) Whether the bookstore provides life insurance benefits

(C) What cashiers need to do when business is slow

(D) How cashiers are included in the business

Answer: Choice (A) incorrectly makes use of the term *die down* to mean "go out of business." Choice (B) takes the same phrase literally, and it plays on the phrase "what else would the . . . job involve?" to mean that the student is asking about job benefits. Choice (D) is incorrect, because it also incorrectly refers to *involve* as meaning "include." Choice (C) is the best answer, because the student is asking what other responsibilities the cashiers would have at the bookstore.

Narrator: Listen again to part of the conversation. Then answer the question.

Manager: Actually, tonight I have to work late to check the stock. Tomorrow'd be just fine. Why don't you stop by here in the morning?

What does the manager want to know?

Ⓐ Whether the student is available to work tomorrow morning

Ⓑ Whether the student will be able to come to the bookstore tomorrow

Ⓒ Why the student is not available the following morning

Ⓓ Why the student doesn't visit the bookstore more often

Answer: With a different tone of voice, and in a different context, choice (A) might be correct. But the manager has not indicated that the student has been hired for the job yet, so (A) is incorrect. Choices (C) and (D) use the *why* question word to tempt you into picking these answer choices, because the manager's question starts with *why*. Choice (C) is incorrect, because the manager doesn't want to know why the student is unable to come—instead the rhetorical function of the question is a suggestion. (D) is incorrect for the same reason; the manager doesn't want to know why the student doesn't come to the bookstore more often. (B) is the correct answer.

Now that you have reviewed the final chapter of listening strategies, let's move on to the final chapter on speaking strategies.

Chapter 16:
Speaking: Summarizing and Synthesizing Review

Remember that in Chapters 4, 8, and 12, we covered the following speaking tasks:

- Describing something from your own experience
- Summarizing a lecture
- Expressing and supporting an opinion based on personal experience
- Summarizing a conversation and expressing an opinion
- Synthesizing and summarizing information

Two separate tasks in the Speaking section require you to synthesize and summarize information, so this chapter also covers:

- Synthesizing and summarizing information

First, let's cover some other important speaking skills and strategies.

Note-Taking

Note taking is a very important skill for the TOEFL, for academic success, and for life in general. We receive a lot of information every day, and we cannot remember all of it. Look at the following conversation:

Michel: Can I get your fax number?

Kathy: Sure. It's area code 3-0-8, then 6-double-9 . . .

Michel: Hang on . . . 3-0-8, 6-6-9 . . . go on . . .

Kathy: No, it's 6-9-9. Not 6-6-9.

Michel: Oh sorry, 6 double 9 . . . and then . . .

Kathy: Then 2-8-3-7.

Michel: Ok, let me read this back: 3-0-8, 6-9-9, 2-8-3-7.

Kathy: You got it!

During this conversation, Michel is taking notes. Answer the following questions.

1. What do you think he will have written down by the end of this conversation?

_____

2. What is the key information?

_____

3. Why does he need that information?

_____

Answers:

1. 308-699-2837

2. The numbers

3. So that he has an accurate fax number for Kathy

You need to be able to identify and take notes on key information. Later, you might use those notes to remind yourself of that information.

PRACTICE: SPEAKING TASKS

There are six tasks in the Speaking section of the TOEFL. The fourth task asks you to read and listen to material on related topics. After reading and listening, you must give a 60-second response to a question about what you read and heard.

Task 4: Synthesizing and Summarizing Information

The fourth task in the Speaking section of the TOEFL is similar to the third task, in that you must read a passage, listen to someone speak on the same topic, and then synthesize and summarize what you have read and heard. However, the third task includes a short announcement followed by a conversation about the announcement, whereas the fourth task includes an academic text followed by a lecture on the same academic topic.

As in the third task, you have 45 seconds to read the passage. You may take notes during the lecture. Then you have 30 seconds to prepare your response to a question that you will see and hear. You then have 60 seconds to respond. On the actual test, you will not see the narrator introduction to the question.

When reading the passage and listening to the talk you should:

- Identify the main points
- Make a note of key words and ideas
- Listen for examples and details that support the main ideas

Following is a sample TOEFL question. Listen to the narrator's introduction. Remember that you will not see the narrator's introduction to the question on the test. If you have a study partner, or someone who can listen to your response, ask that person to read the transcript while you take notes.

⏺ Speaking, Task 4 Narrator

Narrator: In this question, you will read a short passage and listen to a talk about the same topic. After you hear the question, you will have 30 seconds to prepare your response and 60 seconds to speak.

Now read the passage about wolves in Yellowstone Park. You have 45 seconds to read the passage.

Wolves in Yellowstone Park

Wolves once roamed the North American continent from Mexico to the Arctic Circle. However, by 1973, when they were placed on the endangered species list, hunting and trapping had eliminated them from every U.S. state except Alaska and Minnesota. Even the massive Yellowstone National Park was no longer home to wolves.

That changed in 1995 when 14 wolves were reintroduced to the park. Though environmentalists cheered the return of this natural predator to the park, ranchers and farmers whose lands abutted the park protested. They claimed that the wolves would leave the park to prey on their herds. They demanded the right to protect their property and animals from wolves. They even went to court to demand that the wolves be removed.

Notes

Now have a friend read the following lecture transcript to you.

🔊 **Speaking, Task 4 Lecture**

Narrator: Now listen to part of a lecture on this topic in a zoology class.

Professor (male): People who lived near Yellowstone raised a lot of fuss when wolves were returned there by scientists in the mid '90s. The old prejudices and fears came right to the surface again. The "big bad wolf" coming to get you. It's a lot of nonsense really, and the Yellowstone Wolf Project has helped prove that. The wolves are not a problem—in fact, a lack of wolves, or an absence of wolves, is the problem. How many of you have heard of someone being attacked by a wolf? No one, right? Now how many of you know someone who got into a car accident because deer were on the roads or highways? Or have neighbors who can't grow flowers or vegetables because the deer eat everything? Yeah, a lot more of you. We have a serious deer problem in this country because we have no predators to control the deer population. The deer numbers are out of control, but we have people worried about a couple of dozen wolves in Yellowstone. Well, the wolves haven't been causing problems to the neighbors of Yellowstone. Cattle and sheep and horses simply aren't being attacked. The wolves have plenty of deer in the park to keep them busy. We need more wolves—not less.

Notes

● Speaking, Task 4 Prompt

> The professor talks about the results of wolves being
> brought back to Yellowstone National Park. Explain about
> what those results are and how those results are contrary to
> what people living near the park expected.
>
> ---
>
> 30 seconds to prepare   60 seconds to speak

Evaluate yourself using the following criteria:

Criteria	Comments	Action to Improve
Clarity and pronunciation		
Organization		
Details and examples		
Grammar and vocabulary		

Now ask your partner to read the sample response from the transcript. How was it different from yours? How was it similar?

● Speaking, Task 4 Sample Response

Um . . . . Wolves are often seen in movies and other stories as dangerous animals that should be avoided whenever possible. I was surprised when the professor said that more wolves were needed in the park. He said that since because the number of wolves has gone down, the deer population has gone up, because there are no predators to hunt them. He also says that, even though people were afraid that their cows and sheep and horses were going to be attacked, that has not been the case, because the wolves are only hunting deer.

More Practice Synthesizing and Summarizing Information

Following is another sample synthesizing and summarizing TOEFL question. Remember that you will not see the narrator's introduction to the question on the test. If you have a study partner, or someone who can listen to your response, ask him or her to read the transcript while you take notes.

🄜 Speaking, More Practice Narrator

Narrator: In this question, you will read a short passage and listen to a talk about the same topic. After you hear the question, you will have 30 seconds to prepare your response and 60 seconds to speak.

Now read the passage about currency exchange. You have 45 seconds to read the passage.

A Meeting at Bretton Woods

In July 1944, the leaders of 44 nations gathered in a small New England town to set the rules for monetary relations among the major industrialized powers. The most influential countries at Bretton Woods, led by the United States, were united in the belief that a strong international economic system would lead to economic security, which would, in turn, help ensure peace.

As part of their effort to achieve economic stability, the nations gathered at Bretton Woods agreed to maintain fixed exchange rates for their currencies, anchored by the United States's guarantee to redeem international dollar holdings at the rate of $35 per ounce of gold. The Bretton Woods system remained in place relatively unchanged until the early 1970s.

Notes

Now listen to the following Lecture transcript.

🔘 **Speaking, More Practice Lecture**

Narrator: Listen to part of a talk in an economics class.

Professor (male): There are several reasons why the Bretton Woods system eventually broke down. The success of the system depended, to a great extent, on the presence of a dominant player who would be largely responsible for making the rules of the game and making sure those rules were followed. For many years, the United States was that dominant player. Then the 1960s saw Europe and Japan gaining in economic strength, while the U.S. economy, in contrast, got steadily weaker. With inflation rising at home, the United States could no longer claim it's, uh, leadership role, and, uh, eventually, well, the system collapsed when Richard Nixon removed the gold backing from the U.S. dollar in 1971.

But I wouldn't characterize Bretton Woods as a complete failure. It did bring stability to world markets and facilitated increased trade among nations. Indeed, there are some who support a return to the Bretton Woods system in some modified form. Of course, the world is a much different place than it was in 1944. Sixty years ago, no one could have predicted the birth of the euro and the dominant effect its 450-plus million users would have on the world economy. Nevertheless, the fact that Bretton Woods continues to be discussed attests to the very important role that it played in fashioning the world economy after World War II.

Narrator: Now get ready to answer the question.

Notes

🔊 Speaking, More Practice Prompt

> The professor talked about the end of the Bretton Woods system. Explain what the purpose of the Bretton Woods system was and how and why it ended. Give details and examples to support your answer.
>
> 30 seconds to prepare; 60 seconds to speak

Evaluate yourself using the following criteria:

Criteria	Comments	Action to Improve
Clarity and pronunciation		
Organization		
Details and examples		
Grammar and vocabulary		

Now ask your partner to read the sample response from the transcript. How was it different from yours? How was it similar?

🔊 Speaking, More Practice Sample Response

Well, ahh, The Breton Woods system was created at an international meeting in 1944. The meeting was supposed to create standard currency exchange rates between among all of the countries who attended the meeting—this was supposed to create stronger economies, which would then lead to peaceful relations between the countries. The plan was based on the idea that the United StatesU.S. economy was strong enough to support a set value for an ounce of gold. I think it was 35 dollars an ounce. It worked for a while, but the system couldn't last, because in the 1970s, the United StatesU.S. economy wasn't strong enough to keep the dollar value high enough, and President Nixon ended the Breton Woods system.

Congratulations! You have completed all the chapters of Kaplan's Inside the TOEFL iBT. By working through the exercises in this book, you have successfully prepared yourself for all of the different types of questions you may encounter when you take the TOEFL. Good work, and remember to use the skills and strategies you learned is the book on test day!

Part Six
Appendix: Important TOEFL Vocabulary Words

Make sure you are familiar with the definitions of these important words that are used regularly in everyday English language and often appear on the TOEFL. In addition to the form and definition, a sample sentence appears beneath each word to provide context and to clarify its meaning.

abrupt *adjective* sudden

–His abrupt departure surprised everyone.

accentuate *verb* emphasize

–People often choose clothing to accentuate their best features.

acclaim *noun* public praise

–That novel has won a great deal of acclaim both in the United States and in the United Kingdom.

acquaint *verb* become familiar

–To understand a biology text, it's important to acquaint yourself with a number of basic scientific terms.

adhere *verb* stick to

–It is often difficult to adhere to a strict diet.

adverse *adjective* contrary; negative

–Due to adverse weather conditions, the boat races have been canceled.

aesthetic *adjective* pertaining to beauty

–A landscape designer needs to have a good aesthetic sense as well as knowledge of plants.

affect *verb* have an impact on

–Factors such as supply and demand affect the cost of goods and services.

ambiguous *adjective* having two or more meanings; unclear

–His statement was ambiguous, so we still don't know whether he intends to vote yes or no.

ample *adjective* plenty; enough

–There is ample reason to believe that the politician misled the voters.

analogous *adjective* comparable; similar

–The way the immune system works is somewhat analogous to the function of an army.

analyze *verb* study closely; break something down into parts

–Students of cinematic history like to analyze the films of the great directors and discuss their techniques.

anticipate *verb* expect; look forward to

–No one anticipated that Joseph Campbell's work on mythology would become hugely popular.

antiquated *adjective* outdated; obsolete

–The first home computers appear antiquated next to those currently available.

archaic *adjective* ancient; out of date

–The words thou and thee are considered archaic and are no longer used in modern English.

aspect *noun* facet; characteristic; feature

–Religion is a very important aspect of ancient Egyptian culture.

astute *adjective* very perceptive

–Children understand more than one might think, often making surprisingly astute observations about the behavior of adults.

attain *verb* get; acquire

–When a candidate seeks to become the U.S. president, he or she is trying to attain the highest elected seat in the nation.

autonomous *adjective* independent

–Canada has been an autonomous nation for over a century.

avail *verb* make use of

–You should avail yourself of every opportunity to learn.

basis *noun* foundation

–The notion of right and wrong is the basis of morality.

beneficial *adjective* having good effects

–Competition between two businesses can often be beneficial to the customers, as prices may come down.

breadth *noun* width; extent

–The professor's breadth of knowledge was amazing.

bureaucracy noun systems of government administration

–A huge bureaucracy covers laws and regulations relating to employment, education, discrimination, and social welfare.

canon *noun* authoritative list of important works

–Universities are now talking about expanding the canon of literature to include more works by minority writers.

categorize *verb* classify into groups

–Botanists look at several factors to categorize new plant species.

cluster *verb* form a small, tight group

–Many stars cluster together at the center of our galaxy.

collaborate *verb* work together on a project

–Many people find that collaborating on research is easier than doing a project alone.

commercial *adjective* related to business

–Many towns have laws prohibiting commercial activity in areas that are designated as residential.

community *noun* group that interacts with one another in a specific area

  –Some people like to take part in community organizations, such as groups that help the homeless.

complement *noun* something that completes or brings to perfection

  –A colorful scarf can be the perfect complement to a basic wool suit.

complete *verb* finish; add the final pieces

  –Making a timetable and sticking to it is the best way to complete a project on time.

comprehensive *adjective* complete; covering an entire range

  –The book is a comprehensive overview of the field of biochemistry; it covers all the major aspects of the field.

comprise *verb* include; be made up of

  –The United States of America is comprised of 50 states.

compromise *noun* settlement marked by mutual concessions

  –After a great deal of debate, the two sides reached a compromise on the issue.

compute *verb* figure out; determine a number

  –The government uses data from several sources to compute the number of people who need certain services.

concentrate *verb* focus on

  –He gave up painting to concentrate on drawing.

concern *verb* touch on; have to do with

  –The professor's lecture concerns the effects of fossil fuel consumption on the ozone layer.

condition *noun* circumstance

  –People live under different conditions depending on the region in which they live, their age, their class, and their interests.

conference *noun* professional gathering

  –Scientists present their work to their colleagues at conferences.

confidential *adjective* secret; private

  –Though she asked the professor to keep her remarks confidential, he told the head of the department.

conscientious *adjective* careful; ethical

  –He is a very conscientious worker and always does his best on every project.

conservation *noun* protection of natural resources

  –Conservation of natural resources is essential in the world today.

conspicuous *adjective* obvious; easily noticed

  –Though he was hoping no one would notice, his absence from the meeting was conspicuous.

contaminate *verb* to infect by association

–Radioactive waste that is stored in the wrong containers may contaminate the land and water around it.

contemporary *adjective* current; modern

–Contemporary politics is the product of historical elements in politics and other cultural forces.

context *noun* surrounding words or larger situation

–The best way to learn the correct usage of a word is to study it in context rather than in isolation.

conventional *adjective* normal; commonly accepted

–Conventional wisdom says that dogs are more loyal than cats.

convey *verb* carry; express

–A company may spend a great deal of money on advertising designed to convey a specific message.

cornerstone *noun* fundamental component of something

–Belief in democracy is the cornerstone of the American tradition.

cultivate *verb* grow or tend a plant

–In a greenhouse, people can cultivate plants that need special conditions.

cultural *adjective* pertaining to a group's shared beliefs and behaviors

–There are a number of cultural differences between the United States and Europe.

deadline *noun* time when something is due

–The newspaper reporter had to work fast to get the article in by the deadline.

debilitating *adjective* weakening

–A long illness can be very debilitating, leaving the person exhausted even after the illness itself has passed.

deceptive *adjective* false; lying

–A tidepool may appear too small to support aquatic life, but this appearance is often deceptive.

delicate *adjective* fragile

–Delicate plants may die if the temperature changes more than a few degrees.

deplete *verb* to diminish

–If we don't practice conservation, we will deplete our natural resources.

deteriorate *verb* to break down

–After several years of neglect, the building had deteriorated.

dexterity *noun* skill (especially referring to movement)

–He handles the equipment with great dexterity, as if he's had a lot of practice with it.

differentiate *verb* to distinguish; to make or perceive differences

–Not everyone knows how to differentiate between frogs and toads.

dimension *noun* aspect

–Developing the spiritual dimensions of our lives can enrich us.

disregard *verb* ignore

–People should not disregard the warnings on medication purchased at the drugstore.

distract *verb* pull someone's attention away from something

–Automobile drivers may get into accidents if they are distracted by cell phones.

domain *noun* area of authority; sphere of influence

–The scientist said he couldn't explain the event because it lay outside his domain of expertise.

dominate *verb* to be the most important; powerful or authoritative

–Sigmund Freud's views dominated the field of psychotherapy for decades.

dormant *adjective* not active; sleeping

–The volcano at Yellowstone National Park has been dormant since its last eruption 600,000 years ago.

elaborate *adjective* complex; intricate

–An elaborate explanation is not necessary when a short one is sufficient.

elicit *verb* call forth

–The politician's remarks elicited many angry responses.

eliminate *verb* remove

–Vocal coaching can eliminate or reduce a regional accent.

elude *verb* escape capture; move out of reach

–Though he worked on the problem for hours, the answer eluded him.

empathy *noun* understanding for another person

–Children develop empathy gradually, as they mature and learn that other people have feelings.

emphasize *verb* stress; call special attention to

–In written English, italics and underlining are used to emphasize certain words.

enable *verb* make it possible for someone to do

–Knowing the methods of professional historians will enable students to do well later in graduate school.

encompass *verb* include

–Horticulture encompasses many different aspects of the cultivation of plants.

encounter *verb* meet; find

–Students typically encounter a wide range of literary styles in their first year of English studies.

endeavor *noun* attempt; activity

–In any endeavor, the most important key to success is to persist no matter how difficult it may be.

endure *verb* survive

–The great works of literature are those that have endured for centuries.

enhance *verb* improve something's appearance or the experience of something

–The use of dark colors for contrast enhances the beauty of the bright areas.

enrich *verb* add value to

–Schools sometimes offer extra programs, such as music and art, to enrich the students' education.

essential *adjective* absolutely necessary

–Clear pronunciation is essential to making oneself understood.

ethnic *adjective* racial; national or cultural characteristics

–Many large cities in the United States have distinct ethnic neighborhoods where diverse languages and cultures flourish.

evasive *adjective* trying to avoid someone

–He didn't want to admit the truth, so he gave an evasive answer.

evident *adjective* visible; clear

–The hard work he put into his project is evident from the excellent results he achieved.

evolve *verb* develop; change over time

–The film industry has evolved significantly since the early days of silent, black-and-white movies.

exception *noun* special case; one that does not follow the rule

–Grammatical rules often have exceptions that can be confusing to students.

exceptional *adjective* out of the ordinary

–This course will offer students an exceptional opportunity to see a volcano close-up.

exemplify *verb* be an example of

–The movie *The Birds* is often shown to film students to exemplify Alfred Hitchcock's movies.

existence *noun* being

–The existence of videotape recorders has made it possible for people to watch movies in their homes.

extensive *adjective* covering or including a lot

–The university catalog offers an extensive range of literature courses.

fabricate *verb* invent; lie

–It's better to tell the truth than to fabricate a ridiculous excuse.

fallacy *noun* incorrect belief; incorrect way of reasoning

 –Many people believe the fallacy that a correlation between two things proves that one causes the other.

favor *verb* prefer

 –Many artists favor using oil paints rather than watercolors.

feasible *adjective* possible to do

 –It is not economically feasible to provide a computer for every single student in the school.

finite *adjective* limited

 –Physicists argue about whether the universe extends forever or whether it is finite.

fluent *adjective* skilled in a language

 –A fluent speaker of a language understands what is appropriate to say in a given situation.

focus *verb* concentrate on

 –A course in Elizabethan theater typically tends to focus on the works of William Shakespeare.

forfeit *verb* give up; lose

 –An independent contractor may forfeit the right to ask for more money once he or she signs a contract.

formidable *adjective* inspiring a sense of dread

 –The obstacles to completing the project will be formidable, and the project is expected to take several months.

foundation *noun* basis

 –A college education provides a good foundation for professional success.

framework *noun* overall set of guidelines; structure within which something is done

 –Preliminary agreements between two countries can establish a framework within which further agreements can be reached.

genre *noun* style or type of literature or movie

 –The genre of the literature most in demand today is magical realism.

haphazard *adjective* careless; without organization

 –The political protest was not carefully planned but rather put together in a haphazard way.

illicit *adjective* illegal or against moral principles

 –He was charged with several illicit activities.

illuminate *verb* make clear; make understandable

–A close study of the rules by which such governing bodies as the parliament operate illuminates some of their seemingly arcane ways of behavior.

impact *noun* strong effect

–Excessive fishing has had a tremendous impact on the fish population in the ocean.

implication *noun* consequences; additional effects

–Even a small change in the Earth's temperature can have a significant implication for both plant and animal life.

inaccessible *adjective* not available; not reachable

–Some of the world's oil reserves lie so far beneath the ocean as to be utterly inaccessible.

inadvertently *adverb* unintentionally

–The speaker inadvertently offended certain people when he forgot to thank them for their support.

incredible *adjective* impossible to believe; very impressive

–Because of the Earth's different climates, soils, and other growing conditions, there is an incredible variety of plant material.

indiscriminate *adjective* random; without selection

–The soldiers were accused of the indiscriminate killing of civilians.

inevitable *adjective* certain; not avoidable

–The leaders of both countries felt that war was inevitable.

infancy *noun* period of life from birth to about one year

–Children learn an astonishing amount in infancy.

infer *verb* understand something that was not explicitly said

–Careful reading of a passage makes it possible to infer things that were not stated outright.

influence *verb* have an effect on

–The Beatles influenced American music to a great extent.

inhabit *verb* live in

–Many different species of fish inhabit Monterey Bay.

initiate *verb* start

–To help the country out of the Great Depression, President Roosevelt initiated several new social programs.

innovative *adjective* new and creative

–Modern cars feature innovative designs to improve fuel efficiency.

inordinate *adjective*   more than could reasonably be expected

–Drivers have killed an inordinate number of deer on the highways.

integral *adjective*   essential or necessary for completeness

–The 12-note scale is an integral part of the Western musical tradition.

integrated *adjective*   unified; interrelated

–The department offers an integrated curriculum that combines several types of courses.

intense *adjective*   powerful; extreme

–The pain of a knee injury can be quite intense.

keen *adjective*   intense; enthusiastic

–The doctor took a keen interest in new treatments for heart disease.

logical *adjective*   reasoned in a valid manner

–The argument isn't logical, and, therefore, the conclusion is not necessarily true.

manage *verb*   direct; operate

–To manage a company well, it is important to think in terms of both immediate and long-range goals.

mandatory *adjective*   strictly required

–For all members of the orchestra, attendance at rehearsals is mandatory.

manipulate *verb*   handle or work with

–A computer can manipulate numbers much more quickly than a human being can.

mediocre *adjective*   of moderate quality or ability

–Even mediocre film directors are sometimes successful, if they are lucky.

metropolitan *adjective*   urban; relating to a city

–Fortunately, most of the volcanoes in Washington state are far from major metropolitan areas.

myriad *adjective*   innumerable; a vast number of

–The myriad stars in the sky have always inspired people to wonder about what lies beyond our Earth.

narrative *noun*   story

–Filmmakers use a number of devices to clarify story points and ensure that the audience can follow the narrative.

negligible *adjective*   not important

–Doctors were hoping the new drug would have a large effect on cancer, but the effects seem to have been negligible.

obsolete *adjective*   no longer needed

–Computers and printers have mostly made typewriters obsolete.

occupy *verb* be in a place

–The study of subatomic particles occupies a special place in physics.

omit *verb* leave out

–The secretary made a list of the employees but accidentally omitted a few.

original *adjective* new; not copied

–A professor of chemistry is expected to publish the results of original research.

ornamental *adjective* decorative

–Some garden plants are not edible but are strictly ornamental.

physical *adjective* bodily; material

–Ducks and other waterbirds are well suited to live in and around water because of their physical characteristics.

placid *adjective* peaceful; calm

–The placid surface of Lake Superior can easily be stirred up by large storms.

practical *adjective* capable of being put into use

–It is not clear whether cars powered by electricity will ever be practical.

precarious *adjective* very insecure; risky

–Hanging by a single rope, the mountain climber was in a precarious position.

precise *adjective* exact

–Because a computer cannot guess what a person wants, all the instructions given to it must be precise.

predictable *adjective* able to be determined in advance

–Though some people were surprised, most thought that the outcome was entirely predictable.

prerequisite *noun* required knowledge or coursework

–A grasp of basic Japanese is a prerequisite for the intermediate Japanese course.

prevalent *adjective* commonly found

–Cholera was prevalent in London before the invention of modern sewage systems.

profound *adjective* very deep

–The movie *Citizen Kane* had a profound impact on the American film industry.

remarkable *adjective* noteworthy; unusual; impressive

–The Rosetta Stone was one of the most remarkable discoveries in the history of archaeology.

render *verb* depict

–The artist used charcoal and pencil to render the subject.

resilient *adjective* able to recover easily

–Children are surprisingly resilient and heal quickly after an injury.

retain *verb* remember

–Some experts say that experiential learning helps students retain what they learn longer.

reveal *verb* uncover; show

–Films often reveal how cultures see themselves.

rigorous *adjective* strict; careful

–A new drug is subjected to rigorous testing before it is approved for human use.

scrutinize *verb* inspect carefully

–A good teacher can scrutinize a student's performance and give detailed feedback.

significance *noun* importance; meaning

–The discovery of radium had greater significance than most people imagined at the time.

simulate *verb* to create a representation of

–Astronauts are trained in special machines designed to simulate space flight.

spontaneous *adjective* without planning

–The decision to go away for the weekend was spontaneous; no one had even thought about it before.

stimulate *verb* make something happen

–Businesses often have to lower prices to stimulate sales of an item.

subsequent *adjective* following after

–The new drug seemed like to be helpful at first, but subsequent testing showed that it had serious side effects.

subtle *adjective* difficult to perceive; not obvious

–There is a subtle difference between milk from Guernsey cows and milk from Holsteins.

superficial *adjective* not deep

–His discussion of the issues was so superficial, I felt that he barely explained anything.

tactic *noun* maneuver; technique

–Companies often use clever advertising tactics to convince people to buy their products.

tangible *adjective* real; solid; able to be touched

–No one has yet provided tangible evidence of life after death.

tedious *adjective* tiring and boring

–Digging coal is hard, tedious work.

tolerate *verb* to endure

–Most people can tolerate some pain if they know it will end soon.

underestimate *verb* judge something to be smaller or less important than it is

–They underestimated the amount of money needed, and now they have to get the additional funds somewhere else.

universal *adjective* applying to everyone or everything

–The law of gravity is universal.

utilitarian *adjective* emphasizing practicality or usefulness

–The Bauhaus school of architecture emphasized the utilitarian, or functional, aspects of buildings.

vague *adjective* imprecise

–After the accident, he had only a vague memory of what happened.

vast *adjective* immense; very large

–The galaxy is so vast, it is literally impossible for anyone to fully imagine it.

vigorous *adjective* strong; healthy; energetic

–Vigorous exercise is necessary for good health.

waive *verb* relinquish; give up

–Sometimes schools will waive certain fees for students who can show they have limited financial resources.

yield *noun* an amount produced

–The yield of a corn or wheat crop is directly affected by the amount of rainfall that year.

Notes

Notes

Notes

Notes

Notes

Notes

Notes